Who Deserves *Your* Love

Who
Deserves
Your
Love

How to Create Boundaries
to Start, Strengthen, or
End Any Relationship

KC Davis, LPC

Author of *How to Keep House While Drowning*

Simon Element

New York   Amsterdam/Antwerp   London   Toronto   Sydney/Melbourne   New Delhi

SIMON
ELEMENT

An Imprint of Simon & Schuster, LLC
1230 Avenue of the Americas
New York, NY 10020

Author's Note: The stories featured are composites from my personal life and the relationship dynamics I've encountered as a therapist. None are based on any actual client. If I've ever been your therapist, you will not find yourself in my book.

First Simon Element hardcover edition May 2025

SIMON ELEMENT is a trademark of Simon & Schuster, LLC

Simon & Schuster strongly believes in freedom of expression and stands against censorship in all its forms. For more information, visit BooksBelong.com.

For information about special discounts for bulk purchases, please contact Simon & Schuster Special Sales at 1-866-506-1949 or business@simonandschuster.com.

The Simon & Schuster Speakers Bureau can bring authors to your live event. For more information or to book an event, contact the Simon & Schuster Speakers Bureau at 1-866-248-3049 or visit our website at www.simonspeakers.com.

Interior design by Julia Jacintho
Illustrations by Sarah Letteney

Manufactured in the United States of America

1   3   5   7   9   10   8   6   4   2

Library of Congress Cataloging-in-Publication Data has been applied for.

ISBN 978-1-6680-5648-6
ISBN 978-1-6680-5649-3 (ebook)

*For my dad, who kicked the can
down the road pretty damn far.
I love you.*

contents

introduction . . . 01

part one: how to work on your relationships . . . 15

chapter 1: three types of relationship behavior . . . 17

chapter 2: building your advisory team . . . 25

chapter 3: **the vulnerability cycle . . . 31**

chapter 4: how to slow down the vulnerability cycle . . . 41

chapter 5: how emotional dysregulation fuels the vulnerability cycle . . . 59

chapter 6: how to emotionally regulate . . . 69

part two: how to make decisions about relationships . . . 81

chapter 7: compassionate stories do not justify harmful behavior . . . 83

chapter 8: **the relationship decision tree . . . 87**

chapter 9: how to compare your relationship
with others . . . 139

chapter 10: why the small moments matter . . . 147

chapter 11: making decisions with your head and
your heart . . . 155

part three: how to use boundaries to have
better relationships . . . 165

chapter 12: boundaries are the opposite of control . . . 167

chapter 13: boundaries mean being responsible . . . 181

chapter 14: people-pleasing and other
overfunctioning behavior . . . 189

chapter 15: ultimatums and boundaries . . . 201

chapter 16: **using boundaries to stay or disengage . . . 205**

chapter 17: boundaries and abuse . . . 217

chapter 18: the great relay . . . 219

appendix: citations and further resources . . . 223

acknowledgments . . . 229

The quality
of our relationships
determines the quality of
our lives.

—Esther Perel

introduction

This book is a tool that will help you navigate the relationships you have and create the relationships you crave—whether romantic, platonic, or familial. It will guide you to figure out what you want, what you need, and what you can abide by, and how to communicate that to others.

If you are overwhelmed by the idea of reading a whole book but desperately want the information inside, there are two things you can do:

1. **Consider purchasing the audiobook.**
    Some people find that audiobooks are easier for comprehension and attention. I can listen to audiobooks only while cleaning, driving, or doing something with my hands, like puzzles or crocheting. I require stimulation to pay attention.

2. **Read the following selected chapters first.**
    While I believe all the chapters are helpful, if you can read only selected parts of this book, you may want to choose the chapters that lay the groundwork for identifying relationship dynamics that need work and offer specific ways to address them in the following order:

    *   **Finish reading the introduction and chapter 1:**
        This will give you important big-picture information about the goal of this book.

- **Chapters 3 to 4:**
  These chapters cover the Vulnerability Cycle, which helps you identify harmful and reoccurring relationship patterns and provides tools for working on your end of those patterns.

- **Chapters 7 to 8:**
  These chapters outline the Relationship Decision Tree, which is a tool that will help you decide what changes to make in your relationships and why.

- **Chapters 12 to 16:**
  These chapters will introduce you to a new and realistic way to define boundaries that honors the real and nuanced dynamics of life so that you can implement the decisions you have made. They will guide you through a process of finding your own boundaries.

As a therapist who has been working in the mental health field for almost two decades, the majority of my career has been focused on working with individuals who struggle with substance-use disorders and their families. I didn't expect that working in addiction would result in becoming an expert in relationships, but that's what happened. Many people who struggle with addiction turn to substances to cope with painful feelings activated by interpersonal relationships. It follows, then, that developing relationship skills is a key part of recovery, and not just for the substance user. When families and loved ones build better relationship skills, the person with an addiction has a better chance at recovery. So I also developed weekend workshops to help the relatives of people who are addicted identify and address family dynamics that weren't working.

Therefore, an essential component of my practice has always been understanding relationship dynamics. What I've learned about relationships isn't unique to addiction—these dynamics affect everyone. Relationship struggles are universal.

There are lots of books out there about relationship dynamics. My hope is that this book offers a different perspective on how to think about them. "Codependency" is a pop-psychology term that often finds itself in these types of books. But it won't be in this one. That's because codependency often implies that there's a problem in being emotionally dependent on others. Some people then mistakenly believe that true emotional health only occurs when you achieve the Zen-like state of unattachment, as though you need to be able to meet all your own emotional needs yourself.

This is crap. You are a social creature and you need relationships to survive, and you thrive in a state of interdependence. While you are not responsible for meeting every emotional need of another person, you do have *some* responsibilities to others, as they do to you. This book will help you identify which responsibilities are reasonable to meet and which are reasonable to expect. This understanding will be rooted in your own values—not in the demands of others.

Another myth that popular self-help books love to push is that you must love yourself before you accept love from others. This is ridiculous. As you'll see in the stories that follow, so much of my healing emerged from being loved by others! High self-esteem and self-acceptance are not prerequisites for finding deep connection.

You deserve to find a good relationship even if you don't like yourself. Healing our struggles with trauma or insecurity can happen in all kinds of intimate relationships—family relationships, friendships, and romantic partners. Contrary to what society often says, non-romantic relationships are just as valuable as romantic ones.

I would even argue that some issues cannot fully heal outside of relationships. I'm not suggesting that love can magically fix you. Instead, relationships bring issues to the forefront, often painfully, and if you *consciously* use that opportunity, you can work toward healing and growing. This is called conscious co-healing, and the tools in this book can help you achieve it.

Relationships are hard is a common refrain, but what does that really mean? You might think identifying which of your relationship issues are run-of-the-mill difficult and which are actually toxic is perfectly obvious. But it may not be as obvious as you think. The two most common mistakes I see when I work with couples is that a person is either demanding too much or giving too much. But knowing which one you are isn't so easy. Is your mind circling the people you're closest to, trying to assess where you land? How often have you asked yourself, *Am I being unreasonable, or are they being an asshole? Am I being gaslit, or am I the source of the drama?*

Many people have behavior patterns that they may not be fully conscious of—and that may fluctuate according to the relationship. That's why there isn't a uniform approach to interpersonal dynamics. Context is everything. And this book does not do fixed rules. You will not find quippy, one-size-fits-all statements regarding when and how you need to put up hard boundaries.

In my experience, the biggest problem with relationship advice isn't bad advice. It's *good advice* applied *incorrectly.* If two people are in conflict over keeping the house clean, sometimes the problem is that one person is not pulling their weight; sometimes the problem is that one person has unreasonably high standards; sometimes it's the combination of both.

If I offered a blanket statement to never put up with a partner who won't clean the dishes, you'd see that it might be harmful if applied to the second couple, where the issue is that one partner has unreasonably high standards. Good advice for one of these dynamics is not necessarily good advice for all.

My goal is for you to identify the role that each person plays in the dynamics you encounter—to truly diagnose the issue at the heart of the matter—so that you can apply strategies that are appropriate, helpful, and healing.

I may not cover every situation, but I hope to lay the groundwork so that you can apply the lessons with the confidence and knowledge to create the connections you crave.

when it comes to relationships, some of us are set up to fail.

I didn't realize that some of my father's behavior during my childhood was emotional abuse until I was nineteen. I was standing in my college's cafeteria, which held banners about college-wide discussions—from Mental Health Awareness Month to Black History Month to International Women's Day. I never really looked closely at the content on the pillars until my sophomore year.

I remember it vividly:

In the cafeteria are three large pillars. The first pillar is covered with the words "PHYSICAL ABUSE." Underneath there is information on physical abuse and how to get support if you think you have been a victim. Later, when I'm older and have kids of my own, I will come to understand that the spankings I received as a child—where my bare bottom was exposed and struck repeatedly by the hands of my father—constitute physical abuse, but that day I pass the banner without much thought.

Next, I pass the pillar with the words "SEXUAL ABUSE." No one has yet told me that the coercive peer genital touching I experienced during preschool—incidences where the same boy cornered me day after day and pressured me to do things that made me uncomfortable—is not the same as consensual experimentation that happens when kids "play doctor." So I pass this one, too.

And then I see it, the pillar that stops me cold.

EMOTIONAL ABUSE.

I have never heard this term, and yet my stomach tightens and a lump forms in my throat as I read the information: *Emotional abuse is a pattern of behavior where a person controls, isolates, or frightens you in ways that don't include physical contact.*

A list of behaviors that constitute emotional abuse is listed underneath:

- Belittling, name-calling, shaming, and ridiculing

- Threatening violence

- Making someone the subject of jokes, often in front of others

- Questioning memories or reality

- Isolating a person from family and friends

- Engaging in vindictive behavior against another person

- Subjecting others to unpredictable mood swings that cause fear

- Refusing to respect requests to not be touched, even when the touch is not violent

- Not allowing privacy

An additional banner includes a list of behaviors that are specific to the emotional abuse of children:

- Exposing a child to upsetting and age-inappropriate events, such as drug taking

- Withholding affection or comfort from a child as a form of punishment

- Making a child feel unsafe, whether through direct action or lack of action

- Engaging in volatile and unpredictable behavior

My mind automatically highlights the items on the lists that happened to me, and my eyes well with tears. I think of my father.

I love my father, but we had a rocky relationship in my childhood, and the lack of stability did damage. He was emotionally unpredictable largely because of his drinking problem, which caused him to vacillate between being a father who was fun, loving, and affectionate, and someone who was cold, vindictive, and frightening.

I read on: *Emotional abuse creates a traumatizing lack of psychological safety*.

I was not beaten, raped, abandoned, or bullied by my peers. Yet the repeated nature of the emotional abuse that came with living with a father who was addicted to alcohol was traumatizing, and it messed me up.

I wish he would just hit me, so then someone would take me away from here, was something I thought on more than one occasion.

I grew up mistreated just enough to want to be rescued but not mistreated enough to deserve it. I never felt my pain was enough. This one-two punch instilled in me a deep sense of worthlessness that affected my relationships and behavior for years.

I grew up in a home where cruelty was justified when we were angry. I even adopted this mean streak myself at times, not because it brought me pleasure to see someone in pain but because it was a shield that deflected cruelty by lobbing it right back. It was a weapon of desperate defense: *If I can hurt you enough, then maybe you will see how much I am hurting.*

My father and I were locked in a volatile cycle where we constantly triggered and lashed out at each other. I hated him. I loved him. I wanted to punish him. I sobbed myself to sleep after I saw him pour alcohol into a to-go cup that everyone thought was soda—the anger breaking apart under the weight of witnessing my dad in such a sad and vulnerable moment. This dynamic worsened when I developed my own addiction issues as a teenager.

The trauma wasn't just the distressing circumstances of my dad's alcoholism and our volatile relationship. It was also the story that I told myself about *why* it was happening to me: *He does this because he doesn't love me. This is happening because I am broken and unworthy of love.* It was that belief that traumatized me.

I didn't know what was acceptable and what wasn't. This was true when it came to others and in the ways I behaved, too.

Now on the cusp of adulthood, staring up at the words "EMOTIONAL ABUSE," I close my eyes and the tears break the levy of my eyelashes, rolling down my cheeks. Finally, here are words to describe my woundedness.

There, in the middle of the food hall, I finally acknowledge that my pain is enough. What happened to me *was* real. And it was wrong. And, as a result, I developed a belief system about myself and others that forever affected the way I interpreted my relationships.

Another core memory flashes before my eyes.

I am in second grade. My best friend is a thin, shy girl with blond hair and blue eyes. I am a frizzy-haired brunette with painfully pale skin whose loud voice and personality tend to take over the room. We hang out together on the playground. The boys compete to engage with her, and so when she runs, they chase her. Then I chase the boys. Eventually, I lose steam, and the gap between the boys and me widens until I stop completely.

I am standing alone.

I am not good enough to warrant the attention of others.

Is this a preposterous conclusion for a seven-year-old to make? Yes. Is there something ridiculous about a white, conventionally attractive, economically privileged woman claiming that not being chased by boys on a playground was a core memory of being unloved? Absolutely.

What I know now is this: This event did not damage me.

This event did not cause anything.

This event simply highlighted the belief that I had already internalized— about my value, or lack of it—due to the instability in my most important male relationship at home—the one with my father. I believed that I did not deserve love from anyone—especially boys.

the effects of not having psychological safety in relationships

When you experience a pervasive lack of psychological safety in childhood, you learn to hide, suppress, or despise the most vulnerable pieces of yourself because they will be weaponized against you. You hide them to protect yourself, but, in doing so, you ensure that you never get the opportunity to prove the story wrong.

On paper, I was thriving. I had friends. I did well in school. But I always felt like an outsider, secretly afraid that one day my pathetic true self would be discovered and push away any real friends. My fears kept me from finding the right people and caused me to mess up good relationships when I found them.

By junior high, having interpreted every normal childhood experience of hurt feelings or perceived rejection as further proof that I was not good enough, I had an ache, and it was a constant undercurrent in my life. Maddeningly, it was the kind that gnawed on the inside like black mold spreading within the walls of an otherwise well-constructed home. An invisible and lonely pain.

I decided to make this pain manifest into something that would get attention.

I tried self-harm, purging meals, drinking excessively—anything that would get me attention, however negative. Anything that would prompt someone to tell me that they loved me, that they were worried about me. That I was worth worrying about.

None of these schemes worked—I disliked the feeling of puncturing my skin, hated throwing up, and I didn't like the taste of alcohol.

At the beginning of high school, I launched my newest plan. I would be a drug addict. Children who use drugs often find themselves addicted because they slowly become dependent and lose control, desperately wishing they could stop. Not me. When I saw society's adoration of tragic figures like Nirvana's Kurt Cobain, I became convinced that my only chance at love and self-worth was to purposefully run headfirst into addiction and make myself beautifully broken.

Plus, I *loved* doing drugs. Becoming a stoner and a junkie felt like slipping into a custom glove. Relationships were easier. I received attention, affection, and approval and felt deeply connected to others for the first time in my life. I was loved. Finally.

But it was a fleeting kind of love.

I still secretly believed I wasn't worthy of love. But now with several hard drugs in the mix, my feelings were heightened and magnified. If someone was angry with me, it felt like my world was ending. If someone was happy with me, I was euphoric. My moods swung wildly based on how I believed others saw me, and I could not tolerate being alone. It felt like I would cease to exist if I wasn't in the presence of someone else. I hurt good people, and I let bad people hurt me. My relationships felt like a house of cards ready to collapse at any moment.

My addiction to drugs landed me in rehab on the last day of tenth grade. I spent the next eighteen months in inpatient treatment, fighting my addictions.

My experience in the troubled-teen industry is complex. I learned how to identify and talk about my feelings. I discovered and admitted that underneath the bravado, I really hated myself. I also found a community. The way the other girls in the facility embraced and loved me was healing—and I didn't feel so alone anymore. I also had every aspect of my life and body controlled. When I complied and made "therapeutic progress," I was offered praise, acceptance, and basic privileges such as speaking to my family or using the toilet alone. When I did not, there was shame, social isolation, and treatment "exercises" that lasted months, like being forced to carry a bag of bricks or staying silent unless I was given express permission to speak.

This behavior-modification therapy certainly modified my behavior. It put an end to most of my self-destructive behavior. I no longer used drugs or lied or hurt people. I was a productive member of society. But it did not fix what drove the behavior. Although I made healthier choices, my relationships were still driven by a persistent feeling of worthlessness that went back to my relationship with my father.

It wasn't until an interaction with a mentor in a twelve-step program years later that everything cracked wide open for me.

While I was telling her about my father and the trauma related to growing up with an alcoholic—how much he disappointed me, how angry I still was at him for not giving me safety as a child, how I repeatedly attempted to convince him to get sober and apologize—she said four words:

"How old are you?"

"Twenty-two," I responded.

She paused before speaking again. "Your father's responsibility to be the person you needed emotionally when you were a child ended when your childhood did," she said. "I know it's not fair—I know you deserved better. But you can't keep coming back to your father now that you are an adult, expecting him to give you the emotional support you never received—emotional support he isn't capable of right now. You keep going back to an empty well, hoping that there will be something to drink. But the responsibility to heal is now on you."

As painful as this was to hear, it was also incredibly freeing. I had autonomy. I was not reliant on a broken man to change my life. I could heal whether or not my father chose to.

I was only a hostage to my childhood if I decided to be.

I realized that I could reframe my own story: The story could now be that I had a father who was imperfect and who harmed me but who still loved me. Deeply. He always had.

He was a father who had written me a letter every single week I was in rehab (that's nearly eighty weeks), telling me that he believed in me. Some letters were long, written on a legal pad; others were short, a few lines scribbled on a cocktail napkin, even a large piece of paper tablecloth from a restaurant. During a particularly dark week when I wanted to give up, I received a box. It was empty. When I looked closer, I found the contents of a heartfelt letter written on the outside. It was so absurd that I laughed for the first time that week. I was always with him.

I realized that I had to work on reconciling two narratives to show up as an adult in my relationship with him: the father whose addiction traumatized me and the one who always loved me. To change the way that I functioned in relationships moving forward, I had to do two things:

1. Realize that the impact that the trauma had on me was not my fault. Rather, addressing *my behavior* in relationships was my responsibility.

2. Make a decision: Can I learn to love my father for who he is and heal within the relationship as it is? Or is my healing dependent on my putting space between us?

I had to learn from scratch how to balance self-accountability with having standards of behavior for others. I can tell you now that it's a lifelong process. Though I have always been willing to grow, I also recognize that my ability to do so has been massively impacted by the privilege of mental health access and a support system. I have learned not to judge too harshly those who lack the awareness or coping skills that I have.

This is why I've written this book—to share my relearning with people who may not have the access that I've had.

part one

how to work on your relationships

three types of relationship behavior

There are lots of ways to be an ass—here's why that matters.

In a good relationship:
The good times are really good,
And the bad times are *safe*.

Good relationships are not perfect. But they are:

- **Physically safe**

  No one is harming you physically or creating an environment in which you fear they might.

- **Psychologically safe**

  You feel that the person you are engaging with does not wish you harm. You feel safe enough to share your weaknesses without fear that they will be used against you in an intentionally cruel way. You can be open about who you are without fear that the other person will use that openness to punish or humiliate you.

All relationships—friendships, romantic, familial—have good and bad parts. All people have good and bad. But how good is good enough to stay in the relationship? And how bad is bad enough to leave?

Relationships can be hard. Every partnership has conflict, and where there is conflict there are sometimes hurt feelings. People make mistakes. Sometimes they make big ones. Even the best people can be assholes sometimes. But in a good relationship there is a feeling of safety even in challenging times.

Often when you're unfair or unreasonable in a relationship, your reactions can be traced back to some old wound inflicted when you were most vulnerable, before you were able to rationalize what was happening to you. Your past relationship wounds can also cause you to accept unreasonable behaviors from others. These same wounds may cause you to hurt the people closest to you.

I believe that everyone is redeemable. No one forfeits the right to accept love. But many people will behave in ways that make it difficult for others to remain in a relationship with them. That is the consequence of their actions. Some people choose not to be redeemed. Everyone deserves love, but no one is entitled to yours.

Yes, it takes two to tango. But no amount of working on your own imperfections is going to fix a relationship with a person who wants to put you in a choke hold and call it a waltz.

Identifying what kind of a dance you're in is half the battle—and a big part of this book.

To begin to answer that question, we first need to identify and define the three categories of relationship harm:

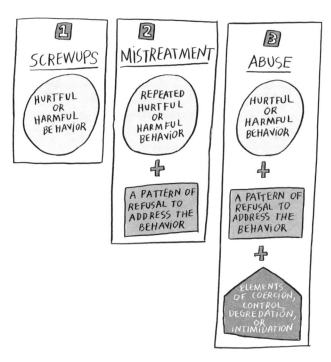

1. Screwups:

    Hurtful or harmful behavior.

2. Mistreatment:

    When a hurtful or harmful behavior is happening over and over, and there is a *pattern of refusal to address the behavior*.

3. Abuse:

    When hurtful or harmful behavior is happening over and over, and there is a refusal to address the behavior, *and there is an element of coercion, control, degradation, or intimidation*.

category 1 behavior:
screwups within equitable (fair) relationships

Even in good relationships, people hurt each other *from time to time*. Sometimes this happens by accident and sometimes on purpose. I call these screwups. I once told my husband to go fuck himself during an argument. A friend forgot about our plans and stood me up for lunch. A relative didn't show up to my baptism because he was under the influence of drugs. One of my friends cheated on his wife once ten years ago.

None of these actions is loving or respectful. They are not acceptable ways to behave, nor do they warrant being easily forgiven and forgotten. I'm simply saying most people have screwed up—often in big ways—and done something damaging or disrespectful to someone they love and respect. An equitable relationship is one where both people admit their mistakes and try to do better *most of the time*.

screwup

If Bill scheduled a weekend boys' trip without consulting his wife, Elaine, who now must care for their three young children alone, that's inconsiderate. It's a screwup. They argue about it, perhaps they raise their voices a bit—maybe Bill sleeps in the guest room—but in the end, they figure out a way to move forward. Maybe Bill apologizes and promises not to schedule big trips without checking in again. Maybe Elaine says that there needs to be some reciprocity in the future, that she would like the opportunity to go away with her friends, which Bill then supports. Whatever way forward, they resolve it. There is give-and-take and collaboration.

category 2 behavior: chronic mistreatment

What happens when someone does something hurtful *repeatedly* and refuses to acknowledge it or refuses to change? This is a different category of behavior.

chronic mistreatment

Compare Bill to Tommy, who goes buck hunting every weekend during hunting season, despite his wife, Nancy, complaining many times that it leaves her to do all the housework and child-rearing. Nancy is worn. She is exhausted. And she tells him so. But Tommy turns his back in a huff and says, "You're the one who begged for kids."

This didn't happen once or twice. Tommy goes off hunting repeatedly without any intention to collaborate on a mutually beneficial solution. It wasn't a one-time screwup or a blowup. It was a pattern of behavior. I refer to this as chronic mistreatment.

In chronic mistreatment, one person is suffering—and is vocal about it—yet the other person either dismisses it or doesn't care enough to change. In some cases, they may apologize but then continue the behavior.

Chronic mistreatment doesn't have to be the exact same behavior repeating—it can also be the same *type* of behavior repeating. For example, if a friend calls me a name during a fight, and we talk about it, but then they stand me up the next week, and I confront them, and then they criticize my appearance a few weeks later, that's still a pattern of mistreatment.

category 3 behavior: abuse

When I speak to audiences about relationships, there are always a handful of people who hear about Tommy, the hunter, and say, "That's abuse!" Perhaps that's what you thought, too. It's true that all abuse is mistreatment, but not all mistreatment is abuse. It's important to define the difference.

Not all forms of abuse are listed. Nor are all examples of abuse easy to spot—abuse often travels under the radar. Defining what constitutes emotional abuse, financial abuse, spiritual abuse, or even covert sexual abuse can be particularly tricky. For example, being hit once is abuse,

abuse

As a therapist, when I see behavior like Tommy's, I look for three things when assessing abusive dynamics:

1. Hurtful or harmful behavior.

2. The repeated occurrence of that behavior with a pattern of refusal to address the behavior.

3. An element of coercion, control, intimidation, or degradation on the part of the person exhibiting that behavior.

Keep in mind that there are some violent behaviors and sexual behaviors that are always abusive **regardless of how frequently they occur**. These behaviors are:

but how many times does someone need to call you a bitch for it to be considered abuse? The answer lies in whether the behavior is a part of a repeated effort to coerce, control, intimidate, or degrade you.

Abuse is never safe.

I am not outlining these three categories of harmful behavior to tell you how to feel about your relationship. The category of chronic mistreatment is not my way of saying it's "not that bad because it's not abuse." On the contrary.

- *Making physical contact with the intent to cause another person bodily injury or pain.* This includes, but is not limited to, hitting, slapping, punching, pushing, grabbing, pinching, or throwing something at you.

- *Intentionally making someone fear bodily injury or pain.* This includes, but is not limited to, grabbing by the collar, raising a fist as if they are about to strike, throwing things near you, or brandishing a weapon.

- *Sexual contact with another person without their consent.* This includes, but is not limited to, touching of genitals or breasts, under or over the clothes, or forcing someone to perform sexual acts.

What I have found in my practice is that many people who are chronically mistreated by their friends, partners, or family members know that something about their relationship is deeply painful but don't quite feel like the label of abuse fits. For them, the recognition that yes, this treatment is abnormal and unreasonable, is very validating.

It is also not my intention to tell you that you are wrong if you define abuse differently than I do. I use "screwups," "mistreatment," and "abuse" to differentiate categories of behavior simply to communicate clearly in this book which advice may or may not be effective for each dynamic. If you are in a relationship where there are elements of control, coercion, degradation, or intimidation, you have unique needs, and some of the relationship advice that is effective in other relationships may be dangerous for you.

Perhaps the most important task ahead is answering this question: How do you approach a relationship where someone is doing their best and their best is hurting you?

To even begin answering it, you are going to need some reinforcements.

the takeaway:

You need to establish the basic standards for a good relationship. You will build from here, but it's essential for you to know what level category of harm exists in your relationship so that you can move forward safely.

building your advisory team

Everyone needs a friend who shows up with margaritas (but maybe don't ask them for relationship advice).

You might think it is perfectly obvious, intuitive even, to know whether your relationship issues are rooted in reasonable struggles or if they are caught up in dynamics that are beyond repair. But in my clinical experience as a therapist, it's not so clear-cut. We all know someone whose partner, friend, or family member seems to lack a baseline respect. *I can't believe they put up with that!* you think. *They deserve so much better!* But they don't see it.

At the same time, I'm sure you can think of a relationship where a friend's expectations are so high that they tend to drop people for the slightest mistake. You might be able to see it clearly. But do they?

Can you clearly describe your own patterns in relationships? So many people cannot. Are you sure you see the other person's behavior accurately?

This book is going to give you a lot to think about it. There will be questions to reflect on, and you might be prompted to make some decisions about your relationships. In my experience, this is most effective when you have a good support system of friends and mentors.

Ideally, you would also have a kick-ass therapist who can help you process. But therapy is not universally accessible—nor are all therapists created equal—and I want this book to be helpful to those who do not necessarily have a good therapist. (Although if your therapist gave you this book, I'm sure that they are wonderful!)

Realistically, most people can get the support they need from a good group of friends or mentors. An Advisory Team is about having a group of people you trust to give you feedback, encourage you, challenge you, and walk you through hard things, such as making difficult decisions. They are the ones who help you understand the relationship with the clarity that some distance often brings.

tips for creating your advisory team

1. **Identify the qualities you need in your Advisory Team:**
    Not every friend needs to be on your Advisory Team, and not everyone on your Advisory Team needs to be a friend. There are going to be people in your life who you love and cherish but who don't have the qualities you need for an Advisory Team—and that's okay! Some members will have some qualities but not others. In general, it's helpful to identify who in your life can do the following:

    - **Validate your feelings.**
      This person is comfortable hearing your raw feelings without trying to fix them. Who in your life can listen empathetically without jumping right in to find solutions or judge you?

- Love you for who you are.

  Even when you are wrong, you still need to feel loved. You want someone who will tell you the truth without shaming you.

- Respect and value you.

  This person lifts you up and believes in your worth. They will embolden you to do scary but necessary things and will light a fire under you.

- Help you achieve clarity.

  This person helps you figure out what you want and what you think rather than just tell you what they think you need to do. They ask good questions that might challenge you to shift your perspective.

- Hold you accountable.

  This person isn't afraid to tell you when you're wrong or when something doesn't sit right with them. They are the ones who call bullshit—who will remind you to check your ego or privilege. They remind you of the value of the word "no." They speak honestly even when the truth hurts. The person who holds you accountable might be the most important person on your Advisory Team.

2. Keep it small:

One mistake people make when they feel they need the input of others is to ask too many people for advice. If you feel the need to consult twenty people about the same issue, it's often because you are hoping you can find someone to give you the "right" answer, i.e., the one you want to hear. But it usually just leads to confusion.

An Advisory Team is a sounding board; it is a group of people who won't help you find the "right" answer but the one that feels authentically right *to your situation.* They are not there so you can take a poll of what everyone else wants you to do.

3. **But not too small:**

    While you don't need to shop every decision around to every person, it's important to create a group wide enough to give you access to a diversity of thought and experience. You want to avoid building an echo chamber. One of the most important outcomes in consulting your Advisory Team is that you gain a shift in perspective or understanding—that you can change your thinking when you need to—and that happens only when you surround yourself with people who are different from you.

    You may want people who are married and people who divorced; people who have great relationships with their parents and people who have more complicated ones; older people and younger people; people with kids and people without them. The wider sample of life experiences the better.

To facilitate honest conversations that might help open you up to different ideas or solutions, I suggest that instead of saying, "Can I get your advice?," try asking, "Can I get your perspective?" This communicates that you don't necessarily need someone to filter their thoughts or to tell you what the right thing is to do. Rather, you are asking them to provide feedback on what they think about the situation.

There are five people in my life who I go to when I need a different perspective or feedback on an issue. But I don't call all five of them when I need to talk something through. I call one or two.

Even my friends who are trained therapists can't always provide me with exactly what I need in that moment. Often I need to tell them explicitly. Sometimes I just need to rant. Sometimes I need someone to tell me when I'm wrong.

My Advisory Team has people I know who will give it to me straight and others who are excellent at validating my feelings. Some are good at many different things on this list. But none fills every single seat. It's important to remember that different people are good at different things—you need all of it, just not from the same person.

You may be thinking to yourself, *KC, I don't have friends like this. Where do I find them?* The answer for how to create meaningful community in your life could be its own book because it can often be difficult. But I can offer you this: Our culture loves to glorify romantic love as inherently more sacred or important than other relationships, but there is nothing wrong with you if you don't have a romantic partner. There is nothing wrong with you if you don't even *want* a romantic partner. Our culture also tells us that it's normal to make big-picture moves for romance; society's prevailing narrative tells us that a great romantic partnership is the most important thing. But this is a flawed narrative. Give yourself permission to create community by making similar dramatic changes, even countercultural ones, for friends and family. Don't be afraid to move jobs, homes, cities even, in pursuit of support. Let yourself get creative and be revolutionary in the pursuit of relationships with friends, extended family, and other community members.

the takeaway:

Every person needs to bounce ideas off other people and get advice from time to time. But it's important to understand how to effectively identify who in your life is going to be helpful when you need relationship advice. These people will be on your Advisory Team.

the vulnerability cycle

Sometimes it feels like you're having the same argument over and over—here's why.

In any relationship, you're responding not only to the other person's behavior, but also reacting to what is going on inside you—your feelings, thoughts, memories, and assumptions. Issues in relationships are almost never about just one person being "wrong" or "bad"—some fixed character flaws—and more about what gets created in relation to another person.

So you must ask yourself this: What reaction is each person contributing to the dynamic? How do you understand the other person's responses? How do you address your own patterns of behavior and take accountability in your own relationship?

To answer these questions, you need to explore relationship dynamics using the Vulnerability Cycle, one of the most important insights I hope you take away from this book. The Vulnerability Cycle is an often unconscious reactive cycle in which each person activates the other in ways that keep you stuck. When you have the same argument over and over. When the substance of the argument may change but something fundamental reoccurs.

marcia and sally

Marcia and Sally are sisters. They share responsibilities for tending to their ailing mother, who has begun to show signs of dementia. Unfortunately, their mother is in denial and resistant to help.

Marcia, the younger sister, feels that she is taking on the lion's share of the caretaking and that Sally doesn't seem to understand the gravity of their mother's situation. Sally, however, feels that Marcia is blowing things out of proportion.

Marcia, who has taken control over their mother's finances after a few out-of-character shopping sprees, believes that their mother would be better served in a nursing home. Sally thinks that their mom is capable of living alone and that it's important to let her live as independently as possible. Sally feels that Marcia focuses on the negative; Marcia feels that Sally isn't facing reality.

As a result, the sisters' relationship has eroded. Let's look now at how each person's combination of sensitivities and defense mechanisms has locked them into a cycle of conflict.

background

Sally, the older sibling, lived most of her childhood in an affluent Dallas suburb, a community focused on keeping up appearances. At the time, her mom stayed at home and her father worked long hours at a law firm. Her parents refused to acknowledge that their marriage was strained by the imbalance of responsibility (her father left all the caretaking of the home and family to her mother). Her parents finally divorced after Sally went away to college.

Marcia is ten years younger than Sally, and she grew up in a completely different environment. Marcia was eight when her parents separated, and she lived with her mother in an apartment in a less affluent suburb than the one in which Sally was raised.

Marcia's childhood was marked by the chaos of divorce: It was not stable, emotionally or financially. Marcia parented her parent, regulating her mother, who was depressed and feeling lost after the separation. Marcia even tackled the practical needs of the household, doing the grocery shopping and cleaning the house. This dynamic created a sense of closeness with her mother. But the responsibility for her well-being was also burdensome. Perhaps it's not surprising that now, as an adult, Marcia is an overachiever who deals with chronic feelings of anxiety by taking charge and exerting her control.

Marcia is sensitive to instability, which is currently triggered by the decline in her mother's health. Watching her mother's inability to care for herself properly brings up feelings for Marcia that activate the childhood stress of being her mother's caretaker before it was appropriate. Marcia's defense mechanisms are to ignore her own needs in service of others, to the point that she becomes aggressive and controlling.

Sally is sensitive to open conflict. Even acknowledging that problems exist makes her uncomfortable. She never learned how to deal proactively with discord. She gets anxious when there's disagreement. Her defense mechanisms are similar to what she grew up with: Ignore the problem until the problem becomes too big to ignore.

sally and marcia's vulnerability cycle

marcia

Marcia begins to construct a story about Sally. She tells herself that *Sally grew up privileged and never struggled. She cares more about staying Mom's favorite than she does actually caring for Mom.* Marcia reacts to this story by taking over and managing the situation.

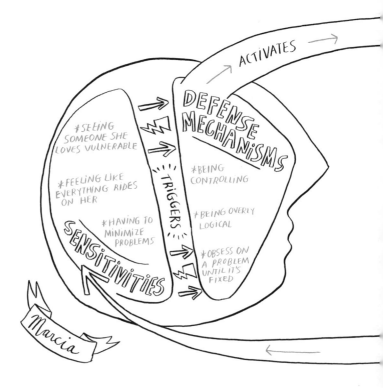

sally

The story Sally tells herself is that *Marcia is so controlling. She thinks I'm stupid and irresponsible. She thinks she is always right and just loves to boss everyone around.* Sally, who is sensitive to open conflict, feels overwhelmed. She reacts to that story by minimizing the problem of their mother's health and avoiding any conversations about it. She begins to screen her sister's calls as a way to suppress her own feelings about her mom's deteriorating health.

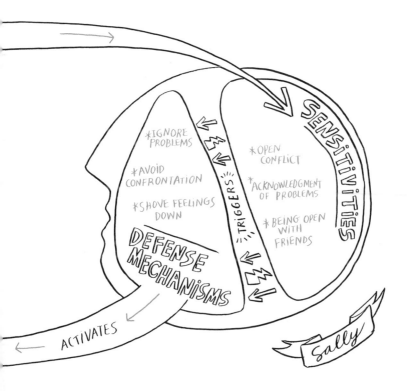

The two are at an impasse. They know their relationship is in trouble. Where do they go from here?

Diving into Marcia and Sally's relationship with the help of the Vulnerability Cycle reveals the moral neutrality of most problems. What I mean by moral neutrality is that in most relationships, there isn't a good guy and a bad guy, someone who is totally right and someone who is totally wrong. There are just two imperfect people activating each other's sensitivities and making emotional decisions. Looking at conflict this way shows us that the blame does not go to one person alone, but rather that two people are in a *system*. They act in relation to each other.

The enemy is not each other but the dynamic that is triggered between them.

sensitivities and defense mechanisms

The first step in the Vulnerability Cycle is to identify sensitivities and defense mechanisms. Your sensitivities kick off your defense mechanisms. Your defense mechanisms activate the other person's sensitivities, which then kicks on their defense mechanisms, which, you guessed it, reactivates your sensitivities. A cycle is born.

Sensitivities are feelings and beliefs from past experiences that emerge during relationship conflict. Sensitivities can be something you are consciously insecure about or feelings that you may be less aware of.

If you grew up with a mother who was emotionally checked out, you may be sensitive to feelings of being ignored. This sensitivity may be activated even if someone isn't intentionally ignoring you. Sensitivities often emerge from the story you tell yourself about what is happening.

If you grew up with unaccommodated ADHD, you may have believed that you were stupid when you struggled with organization or focus in school. As an adult, when a friend teases you about a mistake, even in a fun and loving manner, you may become extra sensitive because of that painful story from your childhood. Others may take the teasing in stride or even find humor in the exchange, but for you, being laughed at opens old wounds. *It touches a nerve.*

It's important to note that sensitivities don't always come from your family of origin; they can also be caused by greater societal factors, including gender experiences or systemic marginalization.

Growing up in a community that did not have access to quality education may make you sensitive to being corrected about the way you say something. Living as a young woman in a culture awash in fetishized female bodies may make you especially sensitive to any discussion of your weight or clothing. Men in our society often suffer from deeply embedded sensitivities about whether they are "man" enough.

Defense mechanisms are ineffective coping skills.

Coping skills are simply the behaviors we developed to deal with adversity. People love to categorize all coping behaviors as "healthy" or "unhealthy." But the reality is that the following are all coping behaviors: journaling, exercising, cocaine, mindfulness, diaphragmatic breathing, masturbation, watching TV, smoking a cigarette, arguing, pushing away your emotions, people-pleasing behavior (the list goes on).

Stop thinking of behaviors as only being good/bad, right/wrong, healthy/unhealthy. Instead, think of all coping behaviors as having a unique cost-benefit analysis. Screaming may work to cope with feelings of anger, but if screaming at your partner damages your relationship and goes against your values, it may be causing more problems than it's solving.

questions for you

**If you are wondering what your sensitivities are,
try completing these sentences:**

I fear I am not good enough because I am _____ .

(stupid/ugly/lazy/too much/et cetera)

I fear I will be rejected for being too _____ .

(emotional/dramatic/boring/et cetera)

My biggest insecurity is _____ .

I will never again let someone else make me feel _____ .

(small/used/thrown away/et cetera)

I tend to react more intensely to behaviors like _____

_____ than other people seem to.

Some ways of coping are frighteningly powerful at turning off painful emotions—things like drinking, drugs, sleeping, or bingeing on food or social media. This doesn't make them immoral or bad. The truth is sometimes you need to stabilize quickly, and harm reduction is always an appropriate priority. But powerful behaviors like this can be tough to regulate in the long term, so it's important to pay close attention to the frequency with which you engage in them and the effects they have on your life.

For example, if you need to scroll TikTok for three hours or drink a glass of wine or eat a bag of cookies after a fight with your mother to stabilize,

If you are wondering what your defense mechanisms are, try answering the following questions:

Whenever someone makes me feel not good enough,
I tend to _____ .

When I feel I'm going to be rejected,
I _____ .

When my insecurities are activated,
I react by doing _____ .

I struggle to change the following behaviors even though
I recognize that I need to _____ .

these can be legitimately effective choices as long as they don't become inflexible patterns that harm you or your relationships.

When you cope with your sensitivities through knee-jerk defense mechanisms, you stay stuck in patterns that harm your relationships.

Let's say because you were bullied as a child, you learned that showing emotions made the bullying worse, so you shut down in the face of adversity. Now, as an adult, you become cold and unfeeling when you perceive any criticism, no matter how valid. This makes for a difficult dynamic with friends and family, who feel they cannot have a productive or challenging conversation without you freezing them out.

If you grew up with a dad who yelled a lot, you may have developed a sensitivity to yelling. When anyone around you yells, it may touch on a deep—often subconscious—fear and discomfort. Your heart rate may accelerate; you may sweat profusely or feel like fleeing the interaction. But you might not know why. Defense mechanisms vary greatly. Your defense mechanism may be to lash out in anger and yell, give someone the silent treatment, or engage in people-pleasing behavior. Whatever strategy you choose, it's often the same strategy you've been using since childhood.

The main factor in whether a coping skill is effective or ineffective is whether you have the ability to *choose* what best fits the situation. For example, ignoring problems can be an effective coping behavior when used flexibly. Perhaps 90 percent of the time, ignoring little things is what keeps the peace in your relationships because you are ignoring stuff you won't care about tomorrow anyway. But if ignoring irritations is the only way you know how to cope with difficult emotions, then it becomes a defense mechanism, and you'll end up ignoring the 10 percent of things that really need to be talked about. As a result, issues will build up until they blow up.

If you find that your defense mechanisms aren't working for you, if they are causing pain and difficulty or causing you to act in ways that don't align with your values, it's time to work on gaining some new coping skills. We'll dive into how to do that in the next chapter.

the takeaway:

No behavior occurs in a vacuum. Just as important as understanding individual issues is understanding the issues created when two people come together.

how to slow down the vulnerability cycle

You can't think your way out of this one.
(Trust me, I've tried.)

In my work as a therapist who specializes in addiction, I've found that substance use is often a defense mechanism in a Vulnerability Cycle. My job is to help clients and families understand how changing the family dynamics can be a powerful tool in achieving and maintaining sobriety.

No one causes another person to use drugs. The decisions around sobriety are solely the responsibility of the person with the addiction. But understanding addiction and in the context of a Vulnerability Cycle can help the family focus on a common goal: how to best support each other by slowing down the cycle. This allows each family member to focus on their own part of the cycle—as opposed to leaning back into blame and defensiveness. This is true of any relationship locked in a Vulnerability Cycle. We can't *cause* someone else to screw up, act selfishly, or engage in hurtful defense mechanisms, but we can look at our own behavior and find ways to better support one another during conflict.

When I ran family therapy workshops, I would first teach families about the Vulnerability Cycle. Then, as they participated in therapy exercises, I would watch that cycle unfold over and over.

But after hours of therapeutic work, the families began to recognize the cycle. They identified their own and others' sensitivities and made the decision to stop engaging in their defense mechanisms.

By the second day, the families were no longer engaging in this cycle. Just kidding! They all came in and did all the same shit the second day.

Maybe—like the dozens of the families I've worked with—you've tried to change the way you act in relationships and still find yourself trapped in the same old cycle. Please don't feel ashamed. You are not broken. It's nearly impossible to stop the cycle with insight alone. You need proactive tools to help your mind *and body*.

Why is that? Why aren't we able to apply this new knowledge about our behavior patterns and just . . . choose to do something different? Because these behavior patterns don't happen as a result of conscious choices—they involve a complex mix of nervous system reactions and subconscious beliefs.

In this chapter, we'll learn more about how we can rewire these nervous system reactions during conflict by challenging the story we tell ourselves.

sarah and devon

Let's apply what we've learned so far about the Vulnerability Cycle to a couple we'll call Sarah and Devon and talk about how they can break their pattern of conflict.

Sarah was ten when her mother died. Her father, who became emotionally absent after his wife's death, dealt with his grief by throwing himself into work, while Sarah struggled to make herself stand out among her three sisters. She learned that to get her father's attention meant that she had to make her needs big and her feelings bigger. She was, her sisters said, "a drama queen."

As a child, Devon learned that the best way to avoid the pain of rejection from his judgmental mother was to stop opening up to her at all. In the face of any unpleasantness, Devon made himself as uninteresting and invisible as possible as to avoid attention from others.

What happens when Devon and Sarah get into a relationship together?

We can visualize each person with their sensitivities on the left side of the circle and defense mechanisms on the right.

For Devon, feeling judged activates his desire to disappear. When he is criticized or feels judged, he shuts down, pulls away, and becomes passive-aggressive (defense mechanisms).

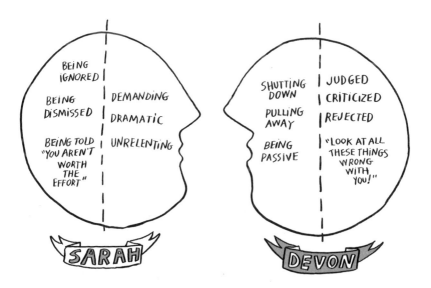

Sarah's sensitivities are feeling ignored or dismissed. She is most sensitive to feeling as though she isn't "worth the effort." When she feels this way, she becomes demanding, dramatic, and unrelenting (defense mechanisms).

The parts of the circles facing each other represent the behaviors each can see, while the parts that are in the back are sensitivities that cannot be seen. These internal struggles are driving their external responses.

Let's go through a scenario where Devon and Sarah experience conflict. As the story unfolds, see if you can identify the following:

- When sensitivities are activated.

- What defense mechanisms each uses.

- The story each person tells themselves. And how that story fuels their responses. This is the most important dynamic to recognize because it is the key to understanding why each person exhibits the behavior they do in the cycle.

the fight

Imagine the following scenario: Devon and Sarah have dinner plans to celebrate Sarah's new job promotion. But in the afternoon, Devon's work project blows up, and there's an all-hands meeting in the conference room with the CEO. Preoccupied, Devon loses track of time. Meanwhile, Sarah sits in the restaurant waiting for him. She texts but gets no response. Because they share their locations on their cell phones, she can see he is still at work. Instantly she feels a pit in her stomach. He isn't even on the way—did he forget? Was this not important to him? She tries calling, but he doesn't answer.

As the minutes tick by without any response from Devon, Sarah's heart rate escalates. Sarah reacts by texting over and over, each text angrier than the last.

Back in the conference room, Devon finally realizes what time it is and runs back to his office to get his phone, where he sees five missed phone calls and twenty texts from Sarah. The most recent one reads "WHAT IS WRONG WITH YOU????"

Devon stares blankly at the phone. He freezes for a moment and feels his chest tighten. Then he texts, "Jesus Christ, Sarah. Something happened at work, and I lost track of time. You act like I've murdered your mother."

She calls immediately, and Devon sends her straight to voicemail. He feels sweaty and clammy—like he wants to crawl out of his skin.

Devon does not go to the restaurant; he does not go home. Instead, he heads to the nearest bar. When Sarah sees Devon at a bar via the location app, Sarah becomes irate. Her eyesight grows blurry. She calls him "a coldhearted asshole" in a text and spends the next hour piling Devon's belongings in the front yard at home and bolting shut the front door.

let's take a look behind the curtain

Now let's look at this fight again so we can see the sensitivities and defense mechanisms lurking underneath the surface.

misconstruction of events

sarah

Sarah recognizes that Devon's absence hurts her, but she doesn't appreciate how deep the pain goes. She is extremely sensitive to feeling ignored—a sensitivity born out of a childhood where she often felt forgotten. When she is stood up and then is unable to contact Devon, her sensitivities are activated. Then she does what we all do: **she constructs a story based on Devon's behavior that makes the depth of her pain make sense.** The story is *Devon doesn't care enough to prioritize our dinner together. He doesn't even respect me enough to explain why he was late. He's selfish and coldhearted.*

In response, she blasts him with unrelenting texts to get his attention—to let him know that she will not accept being ignored. She's desperate to be seen.

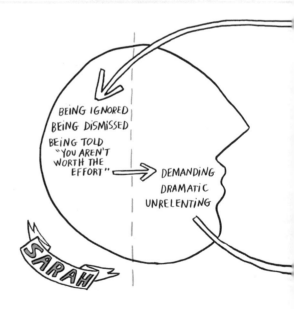

devon

Devon isn't pulling away because he is unfeeling or doesn't care for his partner. Rather, the depth of his panic is overwhelming. This panic activates a sensitivity from deep within his childhood when his mother would criticize him mercilessly and make him feel like a "bad kid" over simple mistakes. Now he subconsciously interprets Sarah's behavior through that same lens. The story he tells himself about Sarah's behavior is *She relentlessly blasted me for a simple mistake, then acted like a psycho and threw my clothes in the yard. I swear if I'm not perfect she punishes me for it.* The only way he knows how to turn off the pain of not being good enough for Sarah is to shut down.

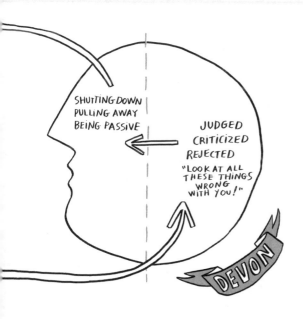

Notice how Devon and Sarah each have a different story about the same event—and neither person here is "good" or "bad." In the face of Sarah's flurry of texts, Devon writes off Sarah as a vengeful drama queen. Faced with Devon's silent treatment, Sarah determines Devon is simply a selfish, unfeeling, "coldhearted asshole."

They are not just reacting to the behavior their partner is exhibiting but also *to the story they are telling themselves*.

If we zoom out for a moment, we can see that this fight is fueled by the Vulnerability Cycle: (1) Sarah's sensitivity to being ignored is activated by Devon's tardiness and lack of communication. She perceives that as an indication that Devon does not care about her. This causes her to grow increasingly aggressive to get the response from him she craves—that he sees her and is not ignoring her, that she matters to him. (2) She projects this anxiety outward and sends him a bunch of texts. (3) The messages activate Devon's sensitivity to being criticized. (4) The angrier Sarah's texts become, the more shut down Devon becomes until he disappears completely—(5) giving Sarah exactly what she feared would happen all along, as she perceives that Devon's unwillingness to engage is a reflection of her not being worth the effort. (6) She reacts to this incredibly painful moment in a way that will force Devon to engage with her by throwing his stuff on the lawn. (7) When Devon comes home to find his belongings strewn about without any regard for his feelings, this confirms what he most fears: that he doesn't matter to Sarah and will never be good enough no matter how hard he tries.

When Sarah and Devon finally talk about the fight days later, they will do what most of us do and defend their actions and blame each other. They might even have another fight that animates the same dynamics: Sarah gets aggressive, critical, and pushy when she feels Devon is disrespectful. He interprets her expressions of hurt as criticism and rejection and becomes avoidant once again—and so the cycle continues.

Not only is each person further activated by the defense mechanisms of the other, but they are also unwittingly participating in the reactivation of their own sensitivities with their own stories about the other person. In fact, the stories they are telling themselves are more hurtful than the harm the other person initially caused.

A key part of slowing down this cycle is to learn how to question the story you tell yourself because of your sensitivities. We aren't trying to abolish the cycle—it's human to have sensitivities and defenses. But if we can identify when the cycle is activated, we can learn to care for ourselves and each other when it happens. This slows down the cycle so it cannot escalate to harmful heights.

In this example, Devon and Sarah really do care for each other. They dislike that their arguments often escalate into hurting each other and are often willing to admit when things go too far.

With that as context, this is a screwup in an otherwise equitable relationship.

Since there is no mistreatment or abuse, they can focus on a common positive goal of discussing what each person is bringing to the relationship dynamic and explore ways they can support themselves and each other.

changing how they speak to themselves and to each other

That first step involves disclosing their sensitivities in a safe and productive way. Instead of knee-jerk defending themselves, Devon and Sarah can spend time seeking to understand where their deep-seated sensitivities emerge from.

Sarah, for example, tells Devon a story about how her father became distant after her mother's death and how, at that same, lonely time, she craved attention. When she didn't get attention, she acted out. Sarah tells Devon, "When you pull away from me, I tell myself it's because you don't think I'm worth the effort of trying. It makes me feel really lonely and afraid."

Devon may find that the story he tells himself about Sarah's behavior— that she's a "drama queen"—changes when he knows where it comes from.

the story devon tells himself

Anytime I make a mistake, Sarah blows it out of proportion and acts like a psycho. On some level she likes when I screw up so she can play the victim.

the new, more accurate story

Anytime Sarah feels ignored or dismissed, she feels like it's just confirmation that she's not worthy of love. She's so scared of being abandoned that she becomes clingy and desperate.

Note: These stories do not justify hurtful or harmful behavior. We are simply taking the first step to understand why each person reacted the way they did.

Sarah also adjusts the story she tells herself about Devon's disregard. Devon tells her about living in fear of not pleasing his mother, who was ruthless with criticism. "My grades weren't good enough, my body was too skinny, my hobbies were weird, the judgment just never ended," Devon says.

the story sarah tells herself

Devon shuts me out when I'm hurting because he doesn't care. He resents me for inconveniencing me with my feelings.

the new, more accurate story

Devon avoids conflict because it makes him feel shame, and he doesn't have the experience to deal with difficult feelings or express them. He fears that I will realize he isn't worth the effort and leave him, so he pulls away first.

Knowing the real reason each person engages the way they do will help them negotiate arguments better and slow down the cycle. Their behavior may still be hurtful, but when they aren't reacting to painful stories they are telling themselves, the distress is much easier to manage.

The other benefit of knowing about this cycle is that Sarah and Devon can learn how they can better care for themselves and each other in high-conflict moments. They may discover that the root of their arguments is that Sarah's sensitivities are activated when Devon pulls away and that Devon's sensitivities are activated when Sarah leans in hard. Now they can discuss what each needs from the other to maintain equilibrium. It might initially look like this:

"I need you to come home and talk to me about this immediately, not go to the bar," Sarah might say. Which will probably prompt Devon to say, "Well, I need you to stop hounding me. I need space!"

Hmm. Well, that's probably not going to work. The goal here is not to force your partner to ignore their sensitivities or just "get over them." In my experience, personally and as a therapist, no matter how emotionally healthy you become, you will likely always have many of the same sensitivities.

This is, believe or not, good news for Sarah and Devon. They don't need to heal all the way to have a better relationship. The scars can remain. Instead, they can learn how to communicate vulnerably about what they need, while still expressing care for the other person. Then they can work together to find mutually beneficial solutions.

these types of conversations can be challenging.
here are some tips to make them more productive.

- Wait until heightened emotions have passed to have a conversation.

- Acknowledge your own sensitivities and take accountability for your behavior.

- Avoid accusations about someone's motives or character and focus on how their behavior impacts you.

- Listen and validate the other person's feelings and sensitivities.

- Emphasize that your goal is a better relationship for the both of you. Invite them to collaborate on solutions that meet both your needs.

When both parties follow these guidelines, a conversation might look like this:

Sarah:

It was wrong of me to call you names and throw your clothes out. I'm sorry. I really struggle when you stop engaging with me when we have a conflict. I feel like what you are saying is that I'm not worth the trouble of figuring it out.

Devon:

That's not what I'm thinking at all. I always think you are worth it. It's me who doesn't feel worth it. I know I messed up, and I feel like one of these days you're going to realize I'm never going to be enough. I just get so overwhelmed I literally can't understand what I'm feeling or thinking, and the more you yell and push me to engage, the more stupid I feel. If you would just give me some space to calm down and think, then I can talk about it.

Sarah:

I'm never thinking you aren't enough, but I can see how it would feel that way when I push so hard. I can give you space to process things, but when you just ghost without a word I'm left wondering, Okay, well, is Devon processing or has he just given up?, and I feel lonely and anxious. Next time you feel overwhelmed and need space, can you just tell me that's what you are doing and let me know when we can talk again? I just need reassurance in that moment you still care and you're still in this.

Devon:

When I missed our date, would it have been more helpful if I had said, "I'm really sorry. I'm feeling overwhelmed by work and now by missing our date, and don't know how to respond. I'm going to take some space to process, and can we talk in the morning? I love you"?

Sarah:

Yeah, I think that would help.

Notice that Devon and Sarah are doing their best to respond with comfort and clarity to the other person's sensitivities rather than defending their actions. Realistically, Devon and Sarah may need some counseling help to get to a vulnerable conversation like this without getting defensive. But the point is that we don't have to become perfectly healed people to slow down the cycle. A few steps toward expressing care to our partner in the midst of conflict goes a long way in slowing down the cycle.

Some people have never engaged in such open and honest conversations and have never developed the emotional skills necessary to do so. That means it's going to be a work in progress—and you'll need to have patience with yourself and the other person. In relationships where both parties are willing to be open and honest, this hard work is worth it. But both parties must be willing to:

- Reflect on how their own beliefs and behavior contribute to the Vulnerability Cycle.

- Collaborate on how they support each other when they both feel activated.

- Take steps to change harmful defense mechanisms.

when vulnerable conversations are not useful or safe

Before we move on to the next chapter, let's get clear about some caveats. Not everyone is willing or able to be open and honest like this, and these kinds of conversations might not be appropriate for every relationship dynamic. There are three key instances in which I do not advise you to attempt having these types of conversations.

not effective:
when someone refuses to look at themselves

If there is a consistent pattern of behavior in which one person is dismissive or hurtful without any intention to change or acknowledge the pain they are causing, then you may be dealing with mistreatment. If someone routinely disregards you, they may not be able or willing to engage in the kind of honest assessment of a relationship that is necessary to do the work to come.

This doesn't need to mean that it's the end of the relationship or that they can't change at all, but it does mean you need to try a different approach. Ultimately you cannot make someone care about you more than they do. Trying to force them into these types of conversations is not going to be effective. Instead, you need to make some decisions about the relationship and implement some boundaries. The chapters to come about the Decision Tree (page 87) and boundaries will help you do this.

not safe:
when abusive dynamics are present

If the other person seems unwilling to examine how their own behavior contributes to the cycle and exhibits behavior that is controlling, degrading, violent, or unsafe, then vulnerable communications are not safe. For example:

• The other person consistently uses your trauma or pain against you. This can look like bringing up the past to embarrass or belittle you when you're trying to engage in thoughtful conversations. It's not a good idea to reveal your sensitivities to this person. They are likely to use that information against you.

- If confrontations ever escalate into violence or the threat of danger. This can look like driving recklessly, threatening to harm you or themselves, or throwing things (these are just some examples). Do not confront them. Protecting your own safety is your highest priority.

If you are in a relationship where the other person exhibits behavior from the list of warning signs of abuse located at the link on page 223, please contact the resources mentioned in the appendix (page 223) so you can ensure your safety before attempting to engage in the Vulnerability Cycle together.

be careful not to confuse safety with a scenario where you may simply feel uncomfortable with your own or the other person's strong feelings.

Safety is about protecting yourself from physical and psychological damage; temporary emotional discomfort is not damage. In other words: It's okay for someone to be angry with you, but it's not okay for them to become violent or to belittle you. Sometimes, because of your own sensitivities, it can feel frightening to hear perfectly appropriate expressions of anger. It is your responsibility to care for your sensitivities—don't use them as an excuse to avoid a difficult, but necessary, conversation.

not appropriate:
coworkers, bosses, acquaintances

There are also everyday relationships that aren't suited for this type of under-the-hood analysis—at least not with the other person. For example, you and your coworker are probably never going to chat about how you activate each other's vulnerabilities, nor would that be a good idea. You don't want to reveal intimate information to a person who has authority over you or a person with whom you don't have a close relationship. You don't want to be in a position where a coworker can use intimate information against you. Nor would you want to hold compromising information about a coworker.

However, when it's inappropriate to have these vulnerable conversations, it can still be powerful to realize that a person's behavior is likely a result of their own insecurities. In other words, you can benefit from the knowledge that there is almost always something behind the curtain that is motivating someone's behavior—and that it's often about them and not about you.

Equally powerful is the realization that your strong reactions may be fueled by vulnerabilities that have nothing to do with the other person. You can still use the tools of emotional regulation in the next chapters to slow down the part of the Vulnerability Cycle that you have control over.

the takeaway:

You don't need to heal all the way to be able to communicate and engage vulnerably in ways that express your needs and respect your partner's needs. You can take control of the stories you tell yourself about the world.

how emotional dysregulation fuels the vulnerability cycle

*Long story short: your brain thinks
your feelings want to kill you.*

So what's up with those recurrent relationship behaviors? Why do some defense mechanisms feel almost compulsive—so difficult to change even when you desperately want to?

It comes down to evolution and a hardwired threat response and how different parts of your brain work together to keep you safe.

- **The survival brain:**

  There is a part of your brain called the amygdala, which links emotions to memories and controls your fight, flight, or freeze response. Let's call it "the survival brain." When your brain perceives a threat, the amygdala floods your brain with stress hormones. This is helpful when you find yourself in urgent physical danger—the stress can heighten your senses and quicken your reaction time. It's also automatic—not something you consciously decide to do.

- **The thinking brain:**

   The part of your brain that is responsible for reasoning, planning, decision-making, and processing cause and effect is housed in your brain's cerebral cortex. Let's call this "the thinking brain." Unlike the survival brain, which is automatic and kicks off reactions unconsciously, the thinking brain allows you to evaluate your feelings and environment and then use your judgment to consciously respond.

The reason that changing your behavior patterns in interpersonal conflict is so difficult has to do with the unique way the survival brain and the thinking brain work—or don't work—together:

The survival brain processes information faster than the thinking brain. Have you ever jumped back or screamed after someone popped out from behind a corner? Even after you realize it's only your roommate, you could probably still feel your heart pumping or the electric feeling of fear. Your brain may have seen that it was your roommate from the very moment she surprised you, so why did it activate a behavioral response that's more appropriate for real danger? It's because your survival brain processes information faster than your thinking brain.

Your survival brain processed *Something is jumping out at me, which is what a predator would do* before your thinking brain realized, *Ah, it's only Susan. She means me no harm.* In those fractions of a second before your thinking brain evaluated the situation, your survival brain had already flooded you with stress hormones and kicked off a reaction that caused your heart to pump, your mouth to scream, and your body to recoil.

why would our brains do that?

Because it's safer. Imagine an early human encountering a tan boulder that looked a lot like a lion. Brains that were hardwired to detect threat first and assess second probably were startled by the boulder and felt a little silly. Those who took the time to assess first and then react didn't get startled by rocks that looked like lions, but they did get eaten by lions that looked like rocks. So the humans who reacted first and assessed second, survived and passed those "startle first, think second" genes onto their kids. In other words, you can thank your ancestors for your anxiety.

1.   **Most of the time, the thinking brain can override the survival brain if it determines the threat isn't real.**
     In the case of your roommate startling you, the thinking brain can often overrule the survival brain and make a conscious decision about how to respond after the initial reaction. Despite being flooded with stress hormones, you can stop yourself from running away or throwing a punch. Your thinking brain communicates to your survival brain that it is a false alarm, so the survival brain ceases to flood the system with stress hormones. You may still need a minute to calm down completely, but you are in control of your decisions and behavior.

2.   **But if the threat is too strong, the survival brain takes over and the thinking brain goes offline.**
     If the threat is real, your survival brain will escalate into full fight, flight, or freeze, which temporarily dampens your connection with your thinking brain. This is because the oxygen needed to power your thinking brain is directed to other parts of your brain and body

that keep you alive—like heightening senses of sight and hearing, dampening senses like pain, and strengthening muscles.

Remember that the survival brain is also responsible for linking emotions and memories. This means that sometimes the thinking brain is unable to override the survival brain because what triggered the threat response is too deeply embedded with a memory of real danger. For most of us, a firework that sounds like a bomb might startle us, but we're able to quickly recalibrate. But for someone who has experienced real bombing, the sound of an explosion may be so deeply linked to the memories of real danger that the threat response is simply too strong for the thinking brain to override. Here the thinking brain cannot stop the physiological fight, flight, or freeze responses. Sometimes this reaction is so severe it causes a major disruption in our mental health and functioning— like with PTSD. But one doesn't have to have PTSD to experience this deep linkage between memory and threat response.

3. **Your survival brain doesn't know the difference between physical threats and emotional threats.**
   There isn't a different region of the brain to process the pain or threat from physical harm versus the pain and threat of emotional harm. The survival brain is just as likely to set off a threat response to rejection and shame as it is to physical intimidation.

4. **Your survival brain does not know the difference between internal and external threats.**
   Just as the survival brain cannot tell the difference between emotional threat and physical threat, it also cannot tell the difference between the pain and fear caused by your own mind and the pain and fear caused by the external world. Thoughts, images, self-

criticism, shame-based memories, and negative predictions all have the potential to set off the survival brain's threat response.

This unique interplay of your survival brain and your thinking brain is why insight alone cannot stop the cycle. Your defensive reactions are governed by your survival brain and all those new fancy coping tools and communication skills are stored in—you guessed it—the thinking brain, which is difficult to access when you feel threatened. The more your sensitivities are activated, the more you disconnect from the thinking brain and make decisions from a defensive stance, the worse the situation gets. This causes you to feel more pain and fear, which activates you even more, making you even more disconnected from your thinking brain. This inability to reconnect with your thinking brain once the survival brain is activated is called being dysregulated.

Pair this experience with another person who is also activated, and you have two dysregulated individuals trapped in a cycle where their emotions and behaviors keep escalating. So, the cycle spins and spins, even as we watch it happen.

Few resources acknowledge how the inability to regulate fuels the Vulnerability Cycle. The reality is that the most distressing emotions are brought on in the context of relationships. And the inability to regulate emotions and behavior drives a great deal of seemingly inescapable conflict.

There are, of course, many states of emotional and physiological activation between total calm and full-blown fight, flight, or freeze states. While there are situations in which the real or perceived threat is so strong a person goes from zero to one hundred in the blink of an eye, such as the veteran with PTSD who hears the fireworks that we mentioned earlier, in most cases the escalation builds over time. If we can learn to recognize the first signs of activation or dysregulation, we can intervene before getting swept up in the cycle.

everyone has three basic levels of regulation.

1.   Comfort zone

When you are regulated, you are in an emotional state that is
equipped to handle challenging situations and life's inevitable
ups and downs. This is your "window of tolerance," where your
brain and body feel safe enough to deal with distressing emotions
or experiences. While you may not always be comfortable in the
comfort zone, you are not losing your shit or completely shutting
down. You are actively engaging with the problem at hand. Think of
yourself in a little sailboat at sea. There may be some bad weather
to deal with, and it may take some effort to navigate the wind and
the waves, but you stay firmly in control of your boat.

2.   Starting to dysregulate

When your sensitivities are strongly provoked, you feel fear and emotional pain. These emotional threats cause the survival brain to release stress hormones. Things begin to get stormy—you may feel overwhelmed, panicky, defensive, reactive, or flustered. Choppy waves and strong winds are rocking your little sailboat. You're still trying to steer, but you're hanging on for dear life. The thinking brain struggles to remain in control as the survival brain begins to take over.

3.   Full-blown fight, flight, or freeze

If your nervous system continues to escalate, you respond in the same way that you would register a physical threat: fight, flight, or freeze. Whether you tend toward fight, flight, or freeze may change depending on the situation. You may experience emotional outbursts, aggression, or erratic or risky behavior (fight). You may physically leave or abruptly disengage from conversation (flight). You may dissociate from your body, emotions, or your surroundings (freeze).

The thinking brain shuts down as the survival brain takes over. As the storm completely overwhelms your sailing capabilities, the wind and waves capsize your boat and you are thrown into the chaotic sea, where you can do nothing but fight to keep your head above water.

How often or quickly someone escalates to dysregulation varies from person to person. Some people can tolerate lots of stress and remain connected to their thinking brain while others might dysregulate quickly over minor issues.

There are neurodevelopmental and mental health disabilities that affect a person's ability to emotionally regulate. A person's boat is greatly affected by childhood experiences, trauma, and access to support, as well as chronic stress, burnout, and oppression. Some people may have a bigger or smaller boat. Waves that might capsize one person might not faze another.

You are not a bad person if you
struggle with emotional regulation.
The size of your boat is morally neutral.
We must steer our boats the best we can.

Ultimately, there is no such thing as becoming so healthy that you never get activated outside your comfort zone. If you have a big boat that allows you to weather most storms without spinning out into fight, flight, or freeze, that's great, but it doesn't make you a better person than someone who does not have the same tolerance. It is morally neutral.

The world is wonderful and painful. There are times when it's legitimate and necessary to feel activated. I doubt it would be possible for anyone to avoid fight, flight, or freeze during a car crash. The goal is not to become a Zen master who remains forever unruffled. It's simply to regain enough behavioral control during heightened emotional states and nervous system arousal that you can make choices that help you, do not harm others, and align with your values and goals.

Perhaps the best news of all is that you can always build a bigger boat. This is an insight that really clicks with my clients. The more you practice the skills of emotional regulation, which we will learn about in the next chapter, the more your boat grows. You won't always struggle as hard as you do now.

the takeaway:

The process of losing connection with your thinking brain is called emotional dysregulation. When you are emotionally dysregulated, your ability to function can be completely overwhelmed by your survival brain, which is dedicated to keeping you alive and safe from danger.

how to emotionally regulate

If I may quote the 1975 cinematic masterpiece Jaws: *"You're gonna need a bigger boat."*

The morning after my husband, Michael, and I had a fight, he got ready for work and left without a word. When he came home, he put the kids to bed and went to his home office to work some more. It wasn't really the silent treatment—we talked about the kids' bedtime logistics as we put them to sleep, a conversation tinged with neither rancor nor tenderness. But the distance, to me, was palpable. I lay in bed, tears welling in my eyes as the pain of feeling alone became too much to bear. The underlying anxiety gnawed at me until I found myself walking into his office, demanding to know why he didn't respond to an earlier text.

Yes, he received it, he said. No, he didn't want to talk about it. I pushed for an answer as to why and laid out my case on the reasons we needed to talk right that instant.

"Because I am angry with you. And I don't want to be angry, and I don't want to talk about it. I just want to work, and I'll eventually not be angry anymore," he said.

The emotional distance and disconnection
made my skin feel like it was on fire.

I demanded we talk then and there, attempting to force the intimacy of argument, and I got my wish. But there was no resolution. I left the argument feeling even more disconnected and lonely.

Since the age of sixteen, my sensitivities were angry men, feeling stupid, and being ignored. These are still my sensitivities, even as I've learned to get healthy around them. A shadow of them always remains.

Part of that growth was learning not to feel shame about my sensitivities. I'm not weak or broken—I'm wounded. We all are. To be human is to be wounded. Life is wounding. And some of us get wounded more deeply than others. All relationships have Vulnerability Cycles and we can't escape them completely.

As I retreated to our room after our discussion, my heart began to pound in my chest, and the panic set in. His displeasure was intolerable. *Can't he see I'm hurting, too? Doesn't he care I'm in pain?* echoed in my heart and mind. The existential dread set in. Everything hurt. Everything was painful. I couldn't stand it.

I knew, of course, exactly what was happening. I knew that his need for space was activating my fears of abandonment rooted in the emotional neglect and trauma of my childhood. Intellectually, I knew that I was safe and loved and that this argument could be overcome. I knew that my husband was neither abandoning nor neglecting me. But this knowledge couldn't fully calm the growing panic that spread through my body. I wanted to run back in. To scream and demand his attention. To make the pain visible in a way that would make him feel compelled to pick me up, hold me, and tell me everything was going to be all right.

But my defense mechanisms of being demanding and frantic would not get me the assurance and security I craved. They never do. I was on the rocky boat and barely hanging on.

This urge to stomp back in and force Michael to understand me was not new to me. Twenty years ago, I was admitted to a psych ward for addiction and had no ability to cope without drugs. I screamed and kicked and clawed there, too, and eventually I learned that it wouldn't get me anywhere, either. I was in for the long haul, and I needed to develop new ways of coping with these overwhelming emotions that ran so deep in my body and brain.

Even after years of practice and education, the panic and pain still sometimes threaten to overtake me.

Lying there on the bed, nearly hyperventilating, I regulated myself with a process I had put together over the years that helps me soothe and calm the survival brain to get the thinking brain back into the driver's seat so I can stop reacting and start responding.

1.   Identify when your sensitivities are activated.

In addition to knowing *what* your sensitivities are and the situations that activate them, it is also helpful to identify behaviors or physiological signs indicating that you feel activated.

For me, it's a panicky feeling, a racing heart, and chest tightening that signal that I am being activated. Just being aware of *when* this is happening can be the signal I need to realize the survival brain is taking over and I need to pause before reacting. You can use the sailboat chart on page 65 to jot down what behaviors or physiological signs can clue you in to each stage of dysregulation.

2.   Stabilize.

Your survival brain may need intervention to stabilize the physiological symptoms of fight or flight and bring your thinking brain back online. Stabilizing exercises often change depending on the situation. Here are a few to begin with.

- Breathe.

  - Box breathing: Breathe in for four seconds, hold for four seconds, exhale for four seconds, and hold for four seconds. Repeat.

  - Slow your breathing and make your exhale longer than your inhale.

- Stimulate your vagus nerve.

  This nerve runs from your brain to your abdomen. When activated, the vagus nerve can lower your heart rate and blood pressure, helping your body relax.

  - Apply a cold compress to your breastbone or the back of your neck. The cold activates the vagus nerve.

  - Drink ice-cold water. Many studies show even something this simple can activate the vagus nerve.

  - Hum. Your vocal chords are connected to the vagus nerve, and humming provides a calming sensation that can activate it and help soothe you back into your window of tolerance.

- Activate the mammalian dive reflex.

  Hold your breath and submerge your face, specifically your nostrils, in very cold water. This submersion exercise lowers your heart rate and increases oxygen to your organs, helping you calm the survival brain and return to your window of tolerance.

- Engage in grounding exercises.

  Look around the room and find five things you hear, four things you see, three things you can touch from where you're sitting, two things you can smell, and one thing you can taste. These all serve to ground and distract you— return you, essentially, back to your body and to your thinking brain.

- Engage in sensory distraction.

    - Eat something sour.

    - Put your hands in cold water and then hot water.

    - Go outside into cold or hot weather.

    - Rock back and forth rhythmically to stimulate your vestibular system, which also soothes and calms your survival brain.

    - Respectfully disengage with someone to give yourself time to regulate.

3.   **Self-soothe: Acknowledge your feelings and give yourself comfort.**

There are many self-compassion exercises and mantras that work to help you regulate. My favorite mantra when I'm feeling upset is to place my hand on my chest and acknowledge, sometimes out loud, *"This hurts. This really hurts."*

When I feel attacked and my fight mode is activated, there is a part of me that wants to scream, *"Fuck you. I'll never let anyone treat me like this again."* This is when I must remind myself of the truth:

- *Just because I feel unsafe doesn't mean I am actually in danger.*

- *Just because someone's behavior feels like an attack doesn't mean it is.*

- *Just because this issue feels urgent doesn't mean I have to do anything right this moment.*

- *Just because I am in emotional pain doesn't mean it won't end.*

4.   **Make room for other stories besides the one that is activating you.**

You can practice making room for other possibilities.

I often have to say to myself directly, "These feelings will not hurt me." I use my thinking brain to question the story I am telling myself about my partner. Is it *really* true that he doesn't care about my pain and that's why he won't engage? Rationally, I know that isn't true. I know he leans out under stress and that he is a person who needs space to process. Maybe we are both just activated at the moment and the whole relationship isn't in the crisis I've convinced myself it is.

Challenging the stories we tell ourselves is important in facing both big issues and in the small moments. I once asked Michael if he could take over unloading the dishwasher every morning so I didn't feel so overwhelmed. When I woke up to find he had left for work without doing it, I was furious. *He doesn't even care that I feel so overwhelmed* was the subconscious story that fueled the long angry text I planned to send. But when I picked up my phone, I discovered he had already texted me: "Shoot, just realized I forgot about the dishwasher. I'm sorry. I'll do it as soon as I get home." The unloaded dishes still inconvenienced me, but he had listened and he did care about me, even though he had made a mistake. This reality was not nearly as painful as the story I was telling myself. Now I try to at least check out the stories I tell myself before reacting to them.

5. Now is the appropriate time for distraction.

As my thinking brain begins to come back online, I find that this is the best time to engage in some distraction. Distraction is not necessarily a defense mechanism. For me, it's key to slowing the cycle. After recognizing that I feel activated, stabilizing my body, pinpointing the stories that are activating me, and making room for new ones, I will take a nap, watch TV, call a friend, do some laundry, take a walk, or go for a drive. Doing the work of self-regulation doesn't mean you stop feeling sad, mad, or disappointed. There is going to be some lingering distress even when your thinking brain is plugged back in. Distraction

a note about psychiatric crisis

Sometimes you are so triggered that you blow right up to the level of a crisis—your red zone. When this happens, you can destabilize to a point that you may enter into a psychiatric crisis.

Signs of destabilizing:

- Hyperventilating

- Blurry vision

- Thoughts of self or other harm

- Feeling outside your body looking down

- Feeling dissociated, or the feeling that nothing is real—that even the most basic aspects of the world around you are an illusion

If you notice these symptoms or begin to feel as though you are in crisis, prioritize interventions that target physiological responses and help you come back into your body safely, such as grounding, vagus nerve stimulation, or sensory distraction. Do not engage in diaphragmatic breathing if you are destabilizing. This can cause hyperventilation and exacerbate the dysregulation.

Speak with a mental health professional if you find yourself dealing with destabilizing states often for a more personalized plan for care. Don't hesitate to call a supportive friend or a crisis hotline if you feel unsafe.

at this point isn't about not feeling your feelings—you aren't trying to become a stoic. On the contrary, real self-regulation means feeling your feelings and still being able to live your life without having to spin out into defense mechanisms or self-destructive habits. Distraction after regulation is about avoiding the temptation to ruminate or obsess (which can reactivate your sensitivities). You feel, and you keep on living.

Distracting yourself at this stage isn't about avoiding conflict. It doesn't mean you won't eventually circle back to the other person to continue important conversations or address inappropriate behavior (both your own and the other person's). It just means you will do it at a time when your thinking is clearer and your emotions are better regulated.

you are only responsible for regulating yourself.

Let's return to Sarah and Devon for a moment. If either of them had practiced emotional regulation and had not engaged in their defense mechanisms, what would have happened to the Vulnerability Cycle that night?

It's possible that in the absence of the long string of insults, Devon wouldn't have felt his sensitivities becoming activated and wouldn't have gone into fight or flight. Still connected to his thinking brain, he may have acknowledged that he had made a mistake by standing Sarah up. Instead of returning Sarah's text with anger, perhaps he would have called and apologized profusely, which may have led to a healing moment of connection between them.

Even if Sarah had still sent those angry texts, Devon could have paused before responding, taken responsibility for his mistake, and ended his own part in the cycle. There's a chance, however, that even if Devon did this, Sarah might still have thrown his clothes on the lawn.

There's no amount of emotional or behavior regulation that can force someone to stop hurting you.

It's not Devon's responsibility to prevent Sarah's emotional escalation—or vice versa. Each person is responsible for their own emotional self-regulation and behavior.

The only part of the cycle you have true control over is the management of your own sensitivities and defense mechanisms. The goal of regulating yourself isn't to try and change the other person, but rather to enjoy greater emotional well-being, which widens your capacity for engaging in meaningful, sometimes challenging exchanges. In some cases, just one person making the decision to change can have a big impact. And this desire to change can be contagious. But it's important to remember that this is not a guarantee.

If Sarah takes steps to understand herself, grows her window of tolerance, and responds differently while inviting Devon to do the same, and Devon does not respond in kind, Sarah is going to have to make some decisions about their relationship.

The next section is designed to help you make those decisions.

the takeaway:

The inability to regulate emotional-threat responses drives a great deal of the repeated conflict in relationships. I've laid out several tools in this chapter that can help you self-regulate so that you can at least step out of the reactivity happening on your side of the cycle.

part two

how to
make decisions
about relationships

compassionate stories do not justify harmful behavior

*Understandable behavior
and acceptable behavior
are not the same thing.*

The Vulnerability Cycle demonstrates that the stories you tell yourself about people are powerful. When you challenge those stories about another person's behavior, you can positively impact your relationships and your ability to emotionally regulate in challenging situations.

Simply making room for the possibility that other stories exist can help slow down the Vulnerability Cycle and make us more open and thoughtful people.

However, sometimes adopting a compassionate story about someone's motives gets us into trouble. Many find it hard to distinguish mistreatment or abuse from garden-variety disagreement. When you challenge your story about *why* the person is harming you, be mindful that you do not *justify* mistreatment by telling yourself things like:

- *He's really trying.*

- *She's doing her best.*

- *She isn't a bad person; she just had a really bad childhood and never learned the skills to be a good mother.*

- *They have a disorder; they can't help it.*

- *He's really sorry.*

Although some of those statements may be true, a better understanding of why people behave in ways that upset or harm you does not mean denying the impact of their actions. It does not mean their behavior is okay. Their actions still have consequences. No one gets a free pass to lose control over their behavior just because they struggle with emotional regulation.

When you change the story that you tell yourself about your mother-in-law, who constantly undermines your parenting in front of your husband and your children, it will look something like this: The initial story: *This woman is a psycho who is out to get me.* The new story: *This woman is terrified of not being the center of her son's world and doesn't have the skills to deal with her own fears of abandonment that have likely been triggered by his transition to adulthood.* The new story doesn't let her off the hook. You aren't saying that her behavior is acceptable or that you aren't allowed to stand up for yourself. Nor are you obligated to heal her or be delicate with her.

Instead, the goal is to stop making yourself the subject of her story. This helps to prevent your own insecurities from being activated by hers. You are adopting a new story that removes you from the center of the narrative. She is not picking on you because you are a bad parent or because she is out to get you personally, but because she struggles with her own insecurities and sensitivities. Now you can decide how *you* want to respond rather than simply reacting. You can stop exhausting yourself trying to gain her approval or taking the bait when she lures you into a power struggle.

Instead of exhibiting a knee-jerk response to your own pain, you are now opened up to the freedom of choices. The choices are not limited to *accept this behavior* or *never speak to her again* but include a spectrum of how (or how not) to engage with this person.

To help you make these decisions—and see a path forward—you need to ask yourself a series of questions, and the Decision Tree can help organize your thinking about what to do next.

the takeaway:

Just because you understand where someone is coming from, doesn't mean you approve of where they're going.

the relationship decision tree

You have the answers. You just needed
someone to give you the right questions.
(You're welcome.)

You've made it this far because someone you care about is exhibiting behavior that is having a hurtful or harmful impact on you. Let's get deeper into it.

If someone has a pattern of hurting you maliciously, simply because they want to be cruel to you, it is always wise to disengage from that person. But it may not always be so obvious whether a person is being purposefully cruel or not.

Sometimes it's more complex. A person may hurt you because they are struggling with their own shit. Maybe they didn't even hurt you on purpose, but they're stressed or suffering or so checked out themselves. Sometimes they're emotionally dysregulated or lacking in important relationship skills. Or perhaps they have a serious cognitive disability that prevents them from even understanding the impacts of their actions. Do you see how difficult it can be to make a decision in these situations? You can understand *why* someone hurts us—and even accept it—but it doesn't stop the pain.

Here are some examples of how complicated it can get.

- Dawn's father has dementia. Despite being a kind father his whole life, the dementia has become so severe that he often becomes angry and verbally abusive to Dawn.

- Beth's friend Tonya has borderline personality disorder. Despite years of therapy, she still pushes away her friends with insulting comments when she feels insecure.

- After losing his mother, David experienced severe depression that he self-medicated with methamphetamines. When anyone in his family confronts his behavior, David lashes out with cruel accusations.

- Byron's boyfriend, Clint, walks away from any heated argument. Anytime there are problems in their relationship, he shuts down and checks out. The next day Clint feels ashamed and lonely.

- When Margot's sister, who has autism, has a meltdown, she often hits anyone who tries to physically interfere. This is difficult for her caregivers, but she cannot control her body when she gets in this state.

- Jamal and Maya have a relationship that is typically tender and casual. But when Jason's combat PTSD is triggered during arguments, he becomes aggressive and may throw things and curse at Maya.

- Jaime and her best friend, Phillipa, have been close their whole lives. But when they get into arguments, Jaime becomes sarcastic. Phillipa is pained by these interactions but also knows that Jaime's parents were verbally and emotionally abusive.

- Mila and Ben both grew up in tumultuous families. When they argue, they engage in name-calling, screaming, and even throwing objects, like plates and remote controls, at each other. They are mostly kind to each other outside of arguments, but they lose all control once fights begin.

That's why relationship advice is hard to generalize. Everyone struggles with something, and most of us want to have empathy and be gracious. But what if someone is doing their best, and their best still hurts us? How long do we work on it? What's reasonable to expect from friends, family, and lovers?

Enter the Decision Tree.

The Decision Tree attempts to put on paper the process that I, as a therapist, would walk a client through to help them make choices in a relationship—stay and work on it or take steps to disengage?

It's not a rigid formula that calculates the right answer about what to do next. Rather, it's a framework for thinking about relationships that helps you reflect on your values to guide you to a decision that you feel good about.

The Decision Tree is not a tool meant to override your feelings or intuition. I'm a big fan of honoring your intuition. But it isn't always that easy. "You'll know when it's right" sounds nice. It may even work for some people. But often the voice of intuition can get lost in a crowd of anxieties and desires. Perhaps your intuition has been damaged by trauma, controlling families, or institutions. You may feel anxious, confused, overwhelmed, or prone to overthinking when trying to determine how you feel.

When your intuition feels less reliable for whatever reason, the Decision Tree offers support and grounding.

Don't ever let anyone make you feel like something is wrong with you just because you need more support. When intuition doesn't seem to provide a clear or trustworthy answer, in addition to relying on your Advisory Team of supportive friends, mentors, or a therapist, the tools in this section can help with clarifying questions that can help you make decisions.

The Decision Tree is designed to give yourself permission to alter your participation in the relationship along one of two general outcomes:

1.   Decide to disengage with the person permanently or temporarily.

2.   Decide to stay in a relationship and implement tools and strategies that protect your well-being.

If you stay, the question is what can you do to make the relationship thrive? If you leave, the question is how do you disengage in a way that is safe *and* honors your values?

The general categories of "stay" or "disengage" are nuanced. There are lots of ways to continue a relationship and lots of ways to disengage from one. Stay does not mean "do nothing" or "accept the behavior" or "keep engaging in the same way as before." Nor does disengage necessarily mean "cut this person off and never speak to them again" (though it sometimes can). Stay means to continue engaging with this person *with boundaries*. Disengage means using boundaries to put some physical or emotional distance between you. Both options require boundaries, which is a topic we will explore in the final section of the book.

the six questions of the decision tree

QUESTION ONE

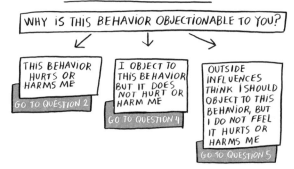

WHY IS THIS BEHAVIOR OBJECTIONABLE TO YOU?

THIS BEHAVIOR HURTS OR HARMS ME
GO TO QUESTION 2

I OBJECT TO THIS BEHAVIOR BUT IT DOES NOT HURT OR HARM ME
GO TO QUESTION 4

OUTSIDE INFLUENCES THINK I SHOULD OBJECT TO THIS BEHAVIOR, BUT I DO NOT FEEL IT HURTS OR HARMS ME
GO TO QUESTION 5

QUESTION TWO

IS THIS PERSON WILLING TO WORK TOWARD COLLABORATIVE SOLUTIONS THAT MITIGATE PAIN?

YES OR UNSURE
GO TO QUESTION 3

NO
SEE OPTION 1

THIS PERSON HAS COGNITIVE DEFICITS THAT MAKE IT IMPOSSIBLE TO GAUGE WHETHER THEY WOULD BE WILLING ABSENT THEIR DISABILITY
GO TO QUESTION 3

QUESTION THREE

DOES THIS PERSON HAVE THE CAPACITY TO LEARN THE SKILLS TO MAKE THE CHANGES NECESSARY?

YES, THEY HAVE THE CAPACITY
GO TO QUESTION 4

I AM UNSURE IF THEY HAVE THE CAPACITY
GO TO QUESTION 4

DUE TO AN INCAPACITATING COGNITIVE BARRIER, PERSON IS NOT CAPABLE OF THE INSIGHT OR BEHAVIORAL CONTROL NECESSARY TO MITIGATE HARM & HURT IN OUR RELATIONSHIP
GO TO QUESTION 4

QUESTION FOUR

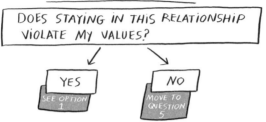

DOES STAYING IN THIS RELATIONSHIP VIOLATE MY VALUES?

YES
SEE OPTION 1

NO
MOVE TO QUESTION 5

QUESTION FIVE

DO YOU WANT TO STAY IN THIS RELATIONSHIP?

YES, I WANT TO MAINTAIN THIS RELATIONSHIP
SEE OPTION 2

NO, I DON'T WANT TO STAY IN THIS RELATIONSHIP
GO TO QUESTION 6

I AM UNSURE IF I WANT TO STAY IN THIS RELATIONSHIP
GO TO QUESTION 6

QUESTION SIX

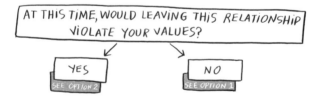

AT THIS TIME, WOULD LEAVING THIS RELATIONSHIP VIOLATE YOUR VALUES?

YES
SEE OPTION 2

NO
SEE OPTION 1

OPTION 1

GIVE YOURSELF PERMISSION TO **DISENGAGE** FROM THIS RELATIONSHIP TEMPORARILY OR PERMANENTLY.

OPTION 2

GIVE YOURSELF PERMISSION TO **STAY** IN THIS RELATIONSHIP & IMPLEMENT BOUNDARIES TO PROTECT YOUR WELL-BEING.

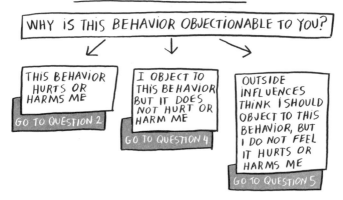

If you are struggling with another person's behavior in a relationship, this is the first question you must answer when you are considering what to do: *Why is this behavior objectionable to me?* This seems like an obvious question, but sometimes it's not so clear-cut. Often, we make decisions about relationships based on what other people say we must feel. But not everyone shares the same values or preferences. A major issue to one person may be a minor inconvenience to someone else.

For example, you may not be bothered that your friend talks about himself all the time and never asks you about yourself, whereas another person would find this behavior self-centered and be tempted to end the relationship over it.

A person whose partner never initiates sex may feel deeply hurt and unseen, while another person whose partner doesn't initiate sex may prefer it that way because of their own trauma history, or because they prefer to be the one to initiate, or simply because they also rarely desire physical intimacy.

A mother who oversteps boundaries can certainly be harmful. But for every family deep in anguish over a controlling matriarch, there is a family playfully rolling their eyes at their obsessively organized, type A mother.

Even when it comes to behavior that seems universally objectionable—like the use of addictive or mind-altering substances—nuances can still exist. A destructive cocaine addiction that causes someone to steal money from family members is clearly a problem, but someone who likes to take hallucinogenic mushrooms once a year at a spiritual retreat may be benign. If the cocaine addiction in question is your partner who lives with you and your children, the harmful impact—the money, the mood swings, the reckless behavior that ensues—is huge. If the person taking mushrooms once a year is your sister, the behavior may not be harmful to you at all. It's just something you object to in principle.

questions for you:
assessing objectionable behavior

Grab a pen and some paper (or any recording device— notes apps or voice memos can work, too) and write down your answers to the following reflection questions. Reach out to your Advisory Team if you need help. Note: If you are at risk of violence in your relationship, please only write your answers down if you can do so safely in a place where they cannot be found.

1. **Is the other person exhibiting behaviors that have you questioning how to handle this relationship?**
   If yes, what are they?

2. **What outside pressures are influencing (or attempting to influence) your decisions about this relationship?**
   For example, your best friend doesn't think your partner is good for you, your therapist is encouraging you to work things out, or your religious leaders say to always forgive. Write down each outside influence and their reasons. Mark which ones you agree or disagree with.

3. **What behaviors, if any, do you find personally objectionable?** Why?

4. **What is the impact of those behaviors on you?**

5. **Which (if any) of your sensitivities are being activated by this person's behavior?**

what next?

After you have answered the above questions, look at the possibilities below. Which one reflects your experience?

- This person's behavior is hurtful or harmful to you. Our example of a person who is hurt by their friend always talking about themselves and never acting interested in the other person falls into this category.
  Move to question TWO.

- You find this person's behavior objectionable, but it doesn't harm or hurt you. Our example of the person who disagrees with their sister's decision to take mushrooms would choose this option.
  Move to question FOUR.

- This person's behavior isn't really an issue for you. You mostly feel as though you *ought to* find it objectionable because of the opinions of outside parties. Someone who does not mind that their partner rarely initiates sex would fall into this category.
  Move to question FIVE.

QUESTION TWO

IS THIS PERSON WILLING TO WORK TOWARD COLLABORATIVE SOLUTIONS THAT MITIGATE PAIN?

YES OR UNSURE
GO TO QUESTION 3

NO
SEE OPTION 1

THIS PERSON HAS COGNITIVE DEFICITS THAT MAKE IT IMPOSSIBLE TO GAUGE WHETHER THEY WOULD BE WILLING ABSENT THEIR DISABILITY
GO TO QUESTION 3

"Mitigating" is the key word in the Decision Tree's second question.

What does that actually mean?

The act of mitigating:

to make something less harmful, unpleasant, or bad

to make less severe or easier to bear

Example:

Getting a lot of sleep and drinking plenty of fluids can *mitigate* the effects of the flu.

In relationships, mitigating means to play an active role in reducing or stopping hurt or harm. But you have to be willing to make some changes.

In most cases, whether the other person is willing to mitigate hurt or harm will eventually come down to action. There will always be people who swear they want to change when they actually have no intention of doing so. They just want to pacify you in the moment. And then there are people who are truly willing to make changes but simply lack the skills to do so.

Willingness can take on many forms, so I think it may be easier to show you what unwillingness can look like. Unwillingness usually has a pattern of placing blame elsewhere.

- "I cheated on you because you wouldn't meet my needs."

- "I hit you because you make me so angry."

- "I called you a bitch because you were acting like one."

- "I stopped talking to you for two days because you made me angry, that's what you get."

When you tell someone that they are hurting you and they blame you for their behavior, you can be certain they are unwilling to do anything different.

But unwillingness isn't always that obvious. Take Lauren and Kim.

Lauren has been struggling with her partner Kim's anger since the beginning of their two-year relationship. When disagreements happen, Kim becomes mean and insulting. Lauren has repeatedly expressed how much Kim's cruel comments hurt her, and Kim has agreed to work on her behavior. She apologizes to Lauren after every fight and goes overboard treating her well afterward. But when Lauren suggests that they go to therapy, Kim says she doesn't have time. Lauren tries to engage in smaller ways. She sees a book about anger and buys it for Kim, who thanks her but leaves it on the nightstand unread. Meanwhile, Lauren continues reading and learns about anger triggers, better techniques on "fighting fair," and communication. Lauren even introduces a concept called *the time-out*, where when an argument gets too heated, they can call a truce and resume the next day as to avoid saying or doing things they don't mean in the heat of the moment. But Kim disregards the suggestion and dismisses it as a silly idea. Kim's only solution is "I'll just stop yelling." But the next time they have a fight, Kim loses her cool and gets mean. This pattern continues. Kim may give lip service about changing but shows no intention to do so.

Remember: Apologizing, being extra nice following an argument, or short-term overtures are not the same thing as being willing to work toward change.

If Kim had gone to therapy, read a book, taken part in conversations where the couple brainstorms together and agrees on ideas about how to deal with anger triggers, Lauren would probably conclude that Kim is willing to mitigate the harm, *even if the anger outbursts keep happening*. Sometimes a person may be trying, but due to lack of support or skills, change is very slow. Later questions in the Decision Tree will help you determine when change is too slow for your needs. Typically, if someone rejects all your suggestions about how you can work on an issue and shows no initiative to come up with their own suggestions, they may be unwilling.

what if the person has a disability?

I use the term "mitigate" instead of "change" here for a very specific reason. In some cases, asking someone to change may make sense. If you're gossiping about your friend, it's reasonable that they might ask you to stop. If you're cheating on your spouse, it's reasonable for them to expect you to end the affair. But asking your bipolar girlfriend if she's willing to change her behavior when she is in a manic state is less reasonable because she has far less control than your gossiping friend or your cheating spouse. Asking your roommate to change his ADHD? Asking your friend to change their autism? Oomph. It gets complicated very quickly.

There's a big difference between asking if someone is willing to stop their disability and asking if someone is willing to work toward mitigating a harmful impact their disability has on you.

Let's say you feel ignored when your husband doesn't look at you when you're talking to him, which makes you feel like what you have to say isn't important. If your husband is neurotypical, the act of mitigating looks like him working on putting his phone down and looking at you when you are speaking to him.

But what if your husband is autistic? For him, making eye contact is distracting and uncomfortable. Is it reasonable to suggest that his love for you is dependent on his ability to change his lack of eye contact? I don't think so. This is why I'm careful to distinguish between mitigation and change.

If your husband is autistic, you might consider changing your story about why your husband doesn't engage in eye contact. With the additional information surrounding his difficulty with eye contact, you might be able to replace the story of *he doesn't care about me* with *he doesn't like eye contact because his brain works differently than mine*.

Sometimes replacing the story isn't enough. If your sensitivity traces back to a childhood wound where you were repeatedly disregarded or dismissed, then the vulnerability may run so deep that the hurt endures. In this case, it's reasonable to ask your spouse for extra support. You can ask yourself *What exactly am I looking for from my husband?*

You see, it's not the eye contact specifically that you need but a signal that *he is paying attention*. Knowing that, you can have a more productive conversation about solutions. Perhaps there are other ways that your husband can signify he is paying attention in a way that works for him. Maybe you need some verbal assent from him, like, "I'm listening, and I care about this." Perhaps you just need dedicated time with him away from electronics. Is he open to a daily walk where you talk and he can keep his eyes on the road ahead of him so that you can both have your needs met?

This is what I mean when I ask, "Is this person willing to work toward collaborative solutions that mitigate hurt or harm?" It's reasonable to expect people you are in relationships with to care about your pain, even when they aren't doing anything "wrong." The point is not whether he necessarily agrees to the exact solution you propose but how he responds to the idea of coming up with a solution that accommodates you both.

This is true if you are the person causing the harm in your relationship. If your ADHD makes it hard for you to maintain your mess and it's having a harmful impact on your roommate, who is overburdened by having to clean up after you, the question isn't *Am I willing to change my ADHD?* Instead, ask, *Am I willing to do things to help lessen the impact of my ADHD on my roommate?*

If you are unwilling to address your messiness because of your disability despite its effect on another person, this shows an unwillingness to address harm. Willingness will look like an openness to explore options. And even if you don't know exactly how best to address the issue, you will not put a hard end to the conversation by brushing it off because it's something that you struggle with because of your disability. Working on a mutually accommodating solution might require some changes from both parties. Perhaps you will go back on your medication, but you will also ask if your roommate can change her weekly cleaning routine to a day when you are both at home so you can clean together.

Keep in mind that it's common for people to initially respond to these conversations by becoming defensive out of embarrassment or shame. If we have done our best to open a productive conversation using the tips from page (52), someone who is willing to work on the relationship will typically come back around for another discussion.

But what happens if the person who is hurting you has severe and consistent cognitive deficits? Maybe your spouse has a brain injury or your mother has dementia. Conditions such as these may make a person incapable of gaining insight into their behavior or engaging in conversations about mitigating harm. If the condition has not been lifelong, you can always reflect upon your previous experiences.

If your spouse, with whom you've enjoyed a loving relationship for thirty years, experiences a traumatic brain injury and becomes aggressive or hurtful, you can draw upon your history. You may conclude that, *yes, if he was not so impaired I know he would be willing to do anything to stop hurting me*. On the other hand, if your mother has always been critical, unkind, and verbally abusive to you, and her dementia diagnosis is exacerbating her cruelty, you may conclude that *even if she had the ability, she would likely be unwilling to be accountable for her behavior*.

The key word in the Decision Tree's second question is "mitigating." It's essential that the person is *willing* to work on changing something about their behavior, even if they deal with disabilities or trauma histories.

questions for you:
assessing willingness

Grab a pen and some paper (or any recording device—notes apps or voice memos can work, too) and write down your answers to these reflection questions.

1. **How does the other person respond when you bring up your feelings and concerns?** Are they understanding, defensive, callous, cold, accusatory, angry . . . ?

2. **How does this person react when they are wrong?** In general, do they show a pattern of willingness to acknowledge when they are wrong?

3. **When it comes to the current issue, what steps have they taken to examine their own behavior?**

4. **How do they explain their behavior?**

5. **How do they respond to invitations to find collaborative solutions?**

6. **What, if any, issues are affecting this person's ability to have insight into their behavior?** These might include trauma, mental health issues, cognitive impairment, and lack of support or emotional skills.

what next?

Once you have reflected on these questions, ask yourself which of these options reflects your experience now.

- This person seems willing to collaborate on mutual solutions and take steps to mitigate harm.
  Move to question THREE.

- You're unsure if this person is truly willing to collaborate on mutual solutions and take steps to mitigate harm.
  Move to question THREE.

- This person has severe cognitive deficits that make it impossible to gauge whether they would be willing to collaborate on mutual solutions and take steps to mitigate harm.
  Move to question THREE.

- This person is unwilling to collaborate on mutual solutions and take steps to mitigate harm. If you feel confident that the other person isn't really interested in addressing the behavior that is causing you so much pain, then it might be time to disengage from that relationship, either permanently or temporarily.
  Move to page (105) to read more about disengaging from a relationship.

what if the decision tree suggests I disengage but . . .

I don't want to?

Remember that there are no "have-tos" in the Decision Tree. The Decision Tree provides prompts that help you *give yourself permission* to disengage. You aren't obligated to work on a relationship where the other person is unwilling to make changes. At the same time, you aren't obligated to leave. The Decision Tree is all about giving you information.

My purpose is not to tell you what to do. My purpose is to give you a tool that will help you to make decisions that you can live with. If you still want to continue in this relationship, I suggest you ask yourself this question: *If this person never becomes willing to make changes, do I still want to be in this relationship?*

You can only make decisions based on the information you have at the time. If you decide to stay, you must be honest with yourself that this decision is made about the person *exactly how they are right now*, not who they used to be or who you hope they might change to be in the future. Change is only possible with willingness.

If you've considered the person as they are now and your answer is still yes, then head over to question FOUR to see if staying in this relationship violates your values.

If staying does not violate your values, you must acknowledge that this person may never be willing to address their behavior. If you still want to stay, then you must own your decision. Do not spend your energy trying to make them willing. Your focus shifts to learning how to create boundaries in this relationship to protect your well-being.

what if the decision tree suggests i disengage but . . .

I'm scared for my safety?

If you're worried that the person you are in a relationship with may become violent or retaliatory if you try to leave, please see the Appendix (page 224) on creating a safety plan and reach out to appropriate resources that I've included. Your safety is paramount. Leaving a relationship like this will take a safe strategy that requires support. The decision to leave has nothing to do with being weak or strong. Whatever way you decide to leave, you deserve safety. We all do.

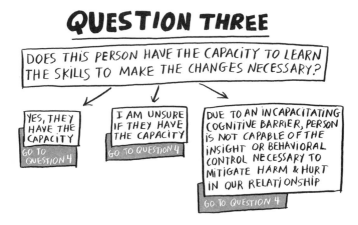

You might be wondering why we explored issues of willingness before issues of ability. Many people assume it's easier to rule out those who cannot change before you examine what to do about people who are simply unwilling to. While that makes sense logically, in my experience as a therapist, it's not as simple as drawing a line between people who can change and those who cannot. When you decide whether someone *can* change before you learn about how to assess whether they are *willing* to change, you often fall into the trap of justifying harmful behavior. This happens because you mistakenly believe (or are told) that the person just can't help it, leading you to put up with hurtful or harmful behavior out of pity or misplaced moral obligation. For this reason, it's more helpful to identify whether you see signs of willingness before you assess capability. That's why we explore willingness first—to avoid the temptation to justify the hurtful behavior of others with the chorus of "Oh, but they can't help it!" This trap is intended to prey upon your compassion.

Thinking about ability in black and white—"they can or they can't"— is not helpful. Let's instead break down behavioral change into three variables: willingness, capability, and skills. Willingness, as we've already learned, is when a person has the motivation to do something; capability is when a person has the potential to do something; and skills is when a person knows how to do something.

For example, let's say two children who don't know how to swim show up to their first day of lessons excited to learn. Jay has a limb difference— his arms were amputated at the shoulders and his legs are amputated at the hips—and Cora is able-bodied. It would be accurate to say that both of these children cannot swim.

Because of the type of limb difference Jay has, he cannot physically propel himself through the water, and there is currently no adaptive equipment that works for his body. Because of this, Jay doesn't have the *capability* to do the breaststroke. No amount of being *willing* to go to swim lessons can change this fact. Cora, on the other hand, has the physical ability to kick her feet and move her arms in a way that is needed to complete the breaststroke. She is *capable* of doing the breaststroke even before that first lesson. What she lacks are *skills*. She must learn how and when to move her legs and arms to propel herself forward. If she is *willing* to continue coming to lessons and practicing, she will learn those skills and soon be able to swim.

Simple, right?

Not quite. We aren't done yet. Let me tell you what happened when I took my two young daughters to their first swim lessons. Both of my children are physically capable of swimming—their arms, legs, and lungs work in ways necessary to making the body swim. But they have different neurodevelopmental processing capabilities. Lila is autistic, and Penny is not. During the first lesson, it became obvious that Lila was having a more difficult time learning the skills than Penny. At the end of the ten sessions, Penny was swimming from one end of the pool to the other, while Lila was still learning to kick off the side and put her face underwater.

We contacted a swim instructor who knew Lila and had experience working with neurodivergent kids. After several weeks using different teaching techniques, Lila gained many more skills. She can now hold her breath underwater for a few seconds and can even push off the stairs and glide a short distance into the arms of her instructor. She still can't swim on her own, but it does appear that she will be able to one day. Her different processing capability doesn't mean she is incapable of learning to swim, it simply means she needs more time and different support to learn the skills.

So, what does learning to swim have to do with changing behavior? As you learned in the chapter on emotional regulation, changing our reactions and behavioral patterns isn't a decision to be made—it's a skill to be learned. And a person's capability to learn new skills affects how difficult— or even possible—that skills-learning process is.

The extent to which that disability affects a person's ability to have insight into and control of their behavior exists on a spectrum. Someone with severe dementia or schizophrenia may experience periods where they have no control over their behavioral symptoms. Other disabilities, such as borderline personality disorder or ADHD, can make it much more difficult, but not impossible, to learn how to choose appropriate behavioral responses. Addiction hijacks the brain in such a way that a person loses control of the ability to stop using, but the degree to which it permanently damages the capability to control their other behaviors long term varies from person to person. Even some trauma can be incapacitating. Having a deeply traumatic experience, especially as a child, disrupts the normal development of important emotional, behavioral, and relational skills.

Not everyone who experiences the same struggles has the same capabilities. Some autistic children do have cognitive or sensory barriers that make them incapable of learning to swim, even if you gave them a thousand lessons. Even though our buddy Jay is incapable of swimming, that doesn't mean all quadruple amputees are. Just ask Ellie Challis, the quadruple amputee who just won gold in the women's fifty-meter backstroke at the Paris 2024 Paralympic Games!

The ability to change is just as affected by one's capacity to change as it is the willingness to change. And one's *capacity* to change is not a reflection on their character or worthiness—it is morally neutral.

As a therapist I can tell you this: addiction, trauma, and disability do not discriminate. Good people with big hearts who want to change sometimes experience morally neutral barriers that make it difficult to regulate their emotions and behavior. No one deserves to be thrown away simply because they are disabled.

But you must also acknowledge that bad actors—real assholes who do not care how their behavior affects you and have no intention of working on themselves—can *also* have disabilities, addiction, or trauma. And those people love to claim that their struggles exempt them from being accountable for their behavior. Do not let anyone do this to you. There is no disability to which the appropriate accommodation is a human punching bag.

Most people have the capacity to learn the skills to mitigate the impact of their behavior on others—even if that behavior is influenced by disability, trauma, or addiction. No one gets a pass to be hurtful and inconsiderate because they have these types of barriers. Except in cases where self-awareness and behavioral control is completely and totally incapacitated, a person must possess, or have at one point possessed, a basic interest in wanting to care for and respect you.

The decision of how to proceed in a relationship with someone who hurts you cannot be based solely on how sympathetic you are to their struggles.

This is true even if you think someone is a good person. Sometimes the behavior of a good person is so damaging that the relationship cannot continue as it is, even if the person "can't help it." It doesn't necessarily mean you cast these relationships aside. It simply means you need to gather more information before you decide how best to proceed.

questions for you:
assessing capability of change

Grab a pen and paper, or any other recording device (and maybe take a breath), and answer these reflection questions.

1. **What stories do you tell yourself about why this person behaves the way they do?**

2. **What things might be making it difficult for them to engage in change or mitigating harmful impact?** Is there anything that might be making it impossible?

3. **Ask a few people on your Advisory Team to listen to the explanations you gave.** Ask them if, in their opinion, you are underestimating or overestimating the other person's capabilities.

4. **When it comes to hurtful or harmful behavior, are you the only person they seem to not be able to control their behavior around?** If so, why do you think that is?

what next?

Once you've reflected on these questions, choose the option that best reflects your current experience.

- Due to an incapacitating cognitive barrier, this person is not capable of the insight or behavioral control necessary to mitigate harm and hurt in the relationship. Your own regulation skills and boundary work may still improve the relationship, but it may not mitigate all the negative impacts of their behavior.
  Move to question FOUR.

- This person has the capability to learn the skills needed to mitigate hurt and harm in the relationship. Since they are both willing and able, this relationship is likely to change for the better.
  Move to question FOUR.

- You are unsure if this person is capable of learning the skills necessary to mitigate the hurt and harm in the relationship.
  Move to question FOUR.

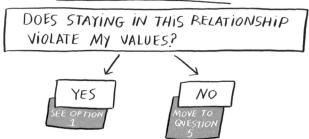

This is the first of two value-based questions we are going to ask ourselves. It's okay if you don't know what your relationship values are yet. You can always borrow mine:

1. Protection and care of minor children.

2. Protection and care of my physical health and safety.

3. Protection and care of my psychological safety (I'm referring specifically to situations in which I am being intimidated, humiliated, controlled, or other harmful behaviors).

4. Intolerance for any dangerous activity that could harm or implicate me or my family.

These are the values that uphold my basic sense of dignity and integrity, and I recommend that you use these when you begin making the list of values that are central to your own self-respect.

A violation of these values is a violation of my humanity. There are no moral, societal, or religious obligations that rise above these fundamental values.

There may be other values that are less universal but equally as important to you. For me, I add two more personal values:

5.   Protection and care of my sobriety.

6.   Protection and care of my elderly parents.

What does this look like in practice? Let's say I've made it this far through the Decision Tree and am now asking myself if staying in this relationship violates my values. Based on my list, remaining in relationships with the following dynamics would violate my values:

1.   Relationships that put my kids in danger of assault, injury, violence, or sexual abuse.

2.   Relationships that lead to environments that allow my kids access to dangerous materials, such as loaded guns or illicit substances.

3.   Relationships that open my kids up to verbal abuse, belittlement, or bullying behavior.

4.   Relationships with someone who subjects any child to danger (even if they aren't mine). For example, engaging in a relationship

with a person who consumes child sexual-abuse material, grooms minors, or deals drugs to children.

5.   Relationships with someone who makes me feel vulnerable to assault, injury, violence, or sexual abuse.

6.   Relationships where someone subjects me to malicious torment.

7.   Relationships that threaten my autonomy (unless I am a threat to myself due to impairment). For example, being told I cannot leave my home, access my money, or make medical decisions for myself.

8.   Relationships that cause me to feel unsafe in my own home. For example, an adult child has relapsed and is breaking into my home or allowing people who are unsafe into my home.

9.   Relationships that implicate me in criminal activity without my consent. This may involve a roommate who is dealing drugs out of our apartment; a boyfriend who keeps stolen goods at our home; a spouse who commits tax fraud; or a friend who shoplifts when we are together.

10.   Relationships that attempt to isolate me from my parents or try to prevent me from taking care of my parents.

questions for you: determing your values

Grab a pen and paper or a recording device and take a moment to write down your own values. Use mine as a starting point.

what next?

Once you've done that, ask yourself if remaining in this relationship at this time violates your values.

- If staying in this relationship doesn't violate your values, move on to question FIVE.

- If staying in a relationship violates your values, give yourself full permission to disengage from it, *even if the other person can't help their behavior.* When fundamental values are violated, it wears away at your humanity and deteriorates your health and well-being. Disengaging is not saying that the other person is unworthy or doesn't deserve love. It is simply saying that supporting their well-being will come at the cost of your own. The important thing to know is that you are not being unreasonable. Your expectations are not too high. You do, in fact, deserve better treatment that is in line with your value system.

Always remember: Our moral obligation to survival is paramount.

Once again, disengaging doesn't always mean leaving permanently. Think of disengaging as leaning out and putting more space between you and that person—whether that space is physical or emotional.

Move on to page (135) to read more about the process of disengagement.

QUESTION FIVE

DO YOU WANT TO STAY IN THIS RELATIONSHIP?

YES, I WANT TO MAINTAIN THIS RELATIONSHIP
SEE OPTION 2

NO, I DON'T WANT TO STAY IN THIS RELATIONSHIP
GO TO QUESTION 6

I AM UNSURE IF I WANT TO STAY IN THIS RELATIONSHIP
GO TO QUESTION 6

Sometimes we just need someone to stop and ask us this directly. If staying does not put you in harm's way or violate your values, you can choose to stay with someone just because you want to, regardless of how difficult the issues are, by implementing boundaries to protect your well-being (which we will explore in the next section).

If your gut is telling you that no, you don't really want to keep dealing with this or if you're unsure, move to question SIX.

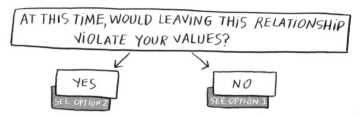

QUESTION SIX

AT THIS TIME, WOULD LEAVING THIS RELATIONSHIP VIOLATE YOUR VALUES?

YES
SEE OPTION 2

NO
SEE OPTION 1

OPTION 1
GIVE YOURSELF PERMISSION TO **DISENGAGE** FROM THIS RELATIONSHIP TEMPORARILY OR PERMANENTLY.

OPTION 2
GIVE YOURSELF PERMISSION TO **STAY** IN THIS RELATIONSHIP & IMPLEMENT BOUNDARIES TO PROTECT YOUR WELL-BEING.

This is where it gets doubly unique to you.

While no one is entitled to a relationship with me, I do have certain responsibilities to people—we all do—and most of the time we can't just disengage without deep consideration. No one wants to go through life discarding important relationships simply because they have become difficult.

But your values are your own. Only you can sort out when behavior becomes so intolerable or hurtful that it nullifies the responsibilities and commitments you have made to someone. In this case, how do you think about whether leaving a relationship violates your values? You can start by exploring further questions:

How close are you to this person?

Most would agree that your responsibility to work things out with your partner of several years is greater than your responsibility to work things out with someone you have dated for a month. The more time you have invested in the relationship, the more effort may be necessary to work on the relationship before disengaging.

If I discover that someone I've just started dating has severe mental health problems and is struggling to function, I would value being honest and kind to them, but I would not necessarily feel it was my responsibility to support them through a major crisis. If I decide that support isn't something I want to offer and I communicate that I am ending the relationship with kindness, I consider myself having met my responsibilities to this person.

However, if my sister develops those same severe mental health problems, it would go against my values to end the relationship completely. That's because I believe my responsibilities to my sister go deeper than honesty and kindness—I have an obligation to support her through difficult times as long as I don't have to sacrifice myself in the process. This also depends on a variety of factors—I might be able to protect and care for myself easily if I see my sister a few times a year. But if I'm living with her, there may not be enough coping mechanisms in the world to keep me safe or sane in that context.

If a friend is rude to me during a conversation, I'm probably not going to end the whole relationship. Dropping a longtime friend over one offense doesn't align with my values. However, if someone I have just met is initially rude to me, then I don't feel any obligation to befriend them. I don't necessarily think they are a *bad person*—they could be lovely and were just having a hard day—but I don't have a responsibility to "work through it" with a stranger or new acquaintance if I don't want to.

what is the level of interdependence in the relationship?

Interdependence is a form of engagement where both people rely on each other in some significant way. This dependence does not have to be equal—one person may offer more than the other. An imbalance in dependence can work when both parties feel loved and fulfilled by the relationship. Disabled individuals exist in interdependent relationships all the time where one has higher needs than the other. Needing more is not the same as unfairly taking more.

People who are in relationships with greater interdependence have usually made more commitments to each other. The higher the level of interdependence in a relationship, the more effort may be necessary to work on the relationship before disengaging. If my husband were to get hit by a bus tomorrow and become unable to function reciprocally in my relationship, my commitment to love him in sickness and in health would compel me to stay. (My love for him is what would primarily drive me, of course, but my point is even if love were not present, there are other values that would guide my decision-making.)

On the other hand, I have a friend I met in rehab. I love her dearly. We spent more than a decade as close friends. She has seen me fall. She has helped me pick up the pieces. There were also times when I did the same for her. But over time, the relationship shifted. Increasingly, our relationship centered around her needs. She started calling only when she was in crisis, often canceled plans at the last minute, and ghosted me for long periods of time, only to remerge when she needed something. It took months before I finally told her directly that our relationship dynamic was hurting me. This upset her, and she hung up. I tried to engage several more times, but she refused. I still love her dearly, and we have spoken occasionally—but I have decided to step back from working on the relationship.

My sense of responsibility to show up and be there for my friend was driven by our shared history—how close we were and how long we had known each other. That's why I spent so long trying to make a friendship work. But eventually, the lack of consideration for my needs combined with the increased demand on my emotional labor affected how long I was responsible for trying to keep the relationship intact.

I want to give you permission to realize the following: You do not have the same responsibility to a family member, partner, or friend who gives very little to you while demanding a disproportionate amount of your time, money, or emotional labor as you do to someone who has consistently shown up for you.

are there spiritual or cultural values that inform your commitment to this relationship?

It is not my intention to tell you to remain in a relationship where you are not happy because of a higher moral principle. I am against the weaponization of religious or cultural morals that force people to adhere to systems of power. I am against unconditional adherence to any religious, spiritual, or cultural mandate out of fear or guilt.

What I am for is respecting your values. Incorporating higher spiritual principles into your value system can be deeply meaningful to you and your community. And I want to acknowledge and respect this decision. *Deeply held religious or cultural beliefs may influence your values and inspire greater effort to work on the relationship before disengaging.*

If staying in your marriage because of the vows you made together in front of your god are more meaningful to you than finding a relationship that has fewer difficulties, then you may decide that leaving violates your values (remember we have already ruled out abusive behavior at this point). If taking care of your aging parents is a cultural code of behavior that you hold dear and you decide to stay in their life, despite various challenges, then I will, of course, support you in that decision.

Again, it's important that the spiritual or cultural values you are using to dictate your decisions are actually your values—ones that make your life feel more meaningful. Not the values that a religious institution or family member has told you that you must adhere to. There is a mighty difference between spiritual and cultural values that bring you purpose and meaning and those that cause fear and shame.

But, KC, when does someone need to disengage regardless of what spiritual or cultural commitments dictate? The answer to that is when staying in the relationship would violate your values, which is why we answered that question first. Remember, there are no moral, societal, or religious obligations that overrule a person's right to physical and psychological safety.

what is the severity of the harm?

Harm exists on a continuum. There are levels of inconsiderate or selfish behavior that you might be willing to tolerate in a person you've known for a long time and are very close to. But these same behaviors might be inappropriate for you to tolerate in new or more casual relationships.

It would not violate my values to end a dating relationship with someone who stood me up on the second date—the harm may be minor in the scheme of things but large enough for me to disengage with them at this stage. Due to the lack of closeness, commitment, or interdependence, I wouldn't feel that I had many responsibilities to this relationship outside of basic respect. I'm not saying it's wrong if I decide to continue a relationship with a person like this; perhaps I really like them and I'm hoping it was just a fluke. I am simply saying that that I have no responsibility to give them a second chance after this kind of infraction. It doesn't make me mean or unreasonable if I decide to not continue this relationship (despite what the other person might think).

If, however, my mother stood me up for lunch, the outcome changes. This relationship has a high level of closeness, commitment, interdependence, and personal/religious values that guide my decisions, so I consider my responsibilities to my mother very high. It would run counter to my values to end my relationship over something like that on its own, even if it turns out she's incapable of ever being on time.

However, *there is a threshold of harm that trumps every other variable*. Consider my relationship with my husband, to whom I also have a high level of responsibility based on closeness, commitment, interdependence, and religious principles. Yet, if my husband cheated on me with my sister, that level of harm nearly zeros out my responsibility to try to work it out. I may still choose to, but I would not feel like I was violating my personal values if I were to walk away after a harm like that.

That threshold is something—like your value system—only you can decide.

would leaving violate my values? my example.

When I moved to Houston, I made a new friend at a baby music class. We hung out a few times during our children's playdates. This friend, let's call her Candace, had a pet-sitting business, and I paid her to watch my cats for a week while I was away. When I got home, the cats' bowls were empty, and the litter box seemed full.

I texted to ask her about it, and she replied that she had been there every day, as she had committed, going so far as to give details of the visit in question. I knew my new friend cared deeply for animals, and I did not believe that she would leave them hungry on purpose, but when I checked my Ring camera footage it was clear she had not come on the last day she was supposed to.

From that point forward, I distanced myself from Candace. Eventually, she asked me why I seemed distant. I told it to her straight: that I had checked my camera and found that she had lied. I told her that the experience had turned me off from our friendship. In response, she apologized and added, "How can you throw away a person for just one mistake?"

It's easy to feel guilted into a decision when someone says something like that. But let's examine this situation according to my own values, rather than her accusations.

I felt conflicted. On the one hand, I value honesty. For many years I have made a point to act with honesty and integrity and have surrounded myself with others who do the same—a decision that has improved my life exponentially. On the other hand, I also value second chances and giving grace for mistakes. Was I being too harsh to end a friendship over one mistake?

Let's use the Decision Tree: Her behavior did hurt me (and my cats!). She promised she would not make the mistake again, so she seemed willing to adjust her behavior. She didn't have any issues that made her incapable of telling the truth. Staying in the relationship would not violate my values. Yet as much as I wanted more local friends, the situation left a bad taste in my mouth.

It all came down to the final question: Would my values be violated if I ended this budding friendship?

1. **What is the depth of the relationship?**
    Consider both the history of the relationship and the closeness you feel.

    I have known this friend for a few months. We are friendly but are mostly at the superficial, new stage of friendship. We see each other at baby class, have had a few playdates, and have texted several times. The depth of this relationship is on the low side.

2. **What is the level of interdependence?**
    How much do you depend on each other? What commitments have you made to one another?

    Because this friendship is still at the superficial stage, we don't depend on each other for anything right now. I have not made any unique commitments to this relationship. Therefore, the level of interdependence is low.

3. **What is the extent of any spiritual or cultural values that dictate your responsibilities to this person?**

    I feel I have a religious responsibility to extend grace and kindness to people. I do forgive her for the mistake and wasn't cruel to her. But none of my important spiritual or cultural values say I have a responsibility to maintain a new friendship.

4. **What is the severity of the harm?**
    How does their behavior affect you? How much damage does their behavior cause?

    Not feeding my animal could have been very harmful—but my cats were okay, just really hungry for a day. Being lied to caused some hurt feelings and damaged trust. I'd say this was mildly harmful.

According to my answers in this assessment, the harm is low, but my responsibility to work on issues in this relationship is also low. I could keep having a relationship with my friend if I wanted to, but it would not violate my values to end this friendship. Ultimately, I decided to end the friendship. Although I desperately wanted friends in my new city, I just didn't enjoy this one after she lied about something so important, and I prefer a friend with more interpersonal skills and maturity.

you don't have to be bad to be wrong (for each other).

Everyone has deep-seated issues. You do, too. When I say deep-seated, I do not mean we are not capable of healing, growth, maturity, repair, and change. I mean that the journey may be long, and there might always be some lingering sensitivities and defense mechanisms that remain in some form.

I have learned that there are just certain people with whom I will never be in a successful relationship. For example, you may have a big heart and a very cool personality, but if you have a tendency to get loud and angry when you are in a conflict, I will probably never choose to get close to you because of my own sensitivities surrounding my father, who was often angry in my childhood and often got loud and angry in our own conflicts. It hurts too bad. It overwhelms my ability to cope too much.

It doesn't mean I think you are bad or unworthy of love— we don't have to demonize someone to decide we cannot be in a relationship with them. It just means our unresolvable issues are not compatible. If leaving a relationship with someone in the "unresolvable issues" category is not a reasonable option, then I enact strong boundaries to protect myself anytime I must interact. And if I can disengage and keep my values intact, then I will.

decision tree example: a spouse's affair

In general, the greater my responsibilities are to a person (based on closeness, interdependence, and cultural or spiritual values), the more effort I am obligated to extend in working on the relationship before ending it. However, this must be weighed against the severity of harm they cause in a relationship.

Let's take another look at an example of using the Decision Tree in a relationship with complex issues.

In most ways, Lola and Stephen have a great relationship. They've been together for fifteen years and consider themselves best friends as well as romantic partners. But after the birth of their first child, their relationship hit some bumps. Lola suffered from severe postpartum depression and, at one point, had to be hospitalized for a week. An outpatient program helped Lola stabilize, and she improved. She incorporated a new fitness routine to help with her mood, and the routine became a passion. Eventually she became a personal trainer and began a job at the local gym, which was a terrific way for her to enjoy her passion for fitness and rediscover her identity—all of which helped her mental health improve.

One frustration for Lola was that when she tried to share her concerns about her mental state, Stephen shut the conversation down, insisting she would probably feel better if she stopped "dwelling on the negative."

Two years ago, Lola's father died suddenly. This was traumatic for her because she had been estranged from her father for more than a decade. At the church where Lola's father worked and worshipped, Lola was groomed and sexually assaulted by a youth pastor. When she told her father, he blamed her. Their relationship never recovered. The grief of her father's death reactivated her trauma, and Lola destabilized. She had sex with one of her trainees at the gym. She confessed to Stephen and showed remorse. She begged Stephen to forgive her. They went to therapy together and learned about their sensitivities, defense mechanisms, and roles in the Vulnerability Cycle. Stephen acknowledged his role in the cycle and started seeing a private therapist to work on being more present in the relationship and more willing to tackle problems as they came, instead of retreating from them. The relationship improved.

But less than a year later, Lola had two more affairs with clients at her gym. This time Stephen discovered her infidelities without her confiding in him first. Now he isn't sure what to do. Stephen truly believes that Lola's sexual behavior is a trauma response. The postpartum depression and the death of her dad destabilized her, and she'd been struggling off and on ever since. He suspects that while she knows she is hurting him, her affair was more a result of her mental health and poor coping skills than of a malicious intent to hurt Stephen. He wants to be sensitive to her struggles, but the affairs caused him to suffer deeply.

Let's watch how Stephen, with the help of his therapist, uses the Decision Tree to help him clarify how he would like to proceed.

1.   Why is this behavior objectionable to Stephen?

Stephen is in extreme pain because of Lola's affairs. Their marriage and friendship are strained, and he doesn't know if he can trust her again.

2.   Is she willing to collaborate on solutions to mitigate the harm?

Lola says she is willing to do anything to save their relationship, including attending couples counseling every week. However, when Stephen suggests that Lola transfer to a new gym or find a new job, she resists. She claims her job helps her with her mental health and that she has a community at her gym. This frustrates Stephen and makes him question her willingness to mitigate harm.

3. Is Lola capable of change?

    Stephen worries that Lola's trauma is so severe that maybe she can't stop her harmful behavior. His therapist reminds him that he isn't asking her to heal completely—just to stop having affairs. The therapist says, "I understand she is in a lot of pain, Stephen, but nobody slips and falls on a dick. She is still in control of her behavior, even if managing her mental health is difficult right now." Stephen reluctantly agrees that Lola is capable of not having sex with men at her gym.

4. At this time, does staying in this relationship violate Stephen's values?

    Stephen examines his list of values:

    1. *Protection and care of minor children.*

    2. *Protection and care of his physical health and safety.*

    3. *Protection and care of his psychological safety (referring specifically to situations in which he is being violated, intimidated, humiliated, or controlled).*

    Stephen determines that his children are safe; Lola continues to be a good mother to them. She does not put him or the kids in physical danger and claims that she has practiced ~~~~~~~~~~ ~~~~~~~ controlling him or implicating ~~~ in ~rime. There is no coercion, intimidating, or violence. Stephen concludes it would not violate his values to stay in the relationship.

4. Does Stephen want to stay?

   Stephen feels conflicted about his marriage. He loves Lola, but he also doesn't want to stay in a relationship with a wife who has extramarital affairs at work.

5. At this time, would leaving this relationship cause Stephen to violate his values?

   Stephen considers his relationship and his responsibilities to Lola.

   1. *He rates the closeness of their relationship as very high.*

   2. *He rates the interdependence of their relationship as very high.*

   3. *He rates the commitment level as very high, since their marriage vows included working through difficult times.*

   4. *He rates spiritual or cultural values as low, because this does not inform his decision.*

   5. *He rates the severity of the harm very high.*

Stephen concludes that he views his responsibilities to work things out with his wife as very high due to their closeness and shared responsibilities, especially as parents. Stephen ultimately decides to stay in the relationship for now, but implements a boundary; he tells Lola that if she has another affair, he will have to end their marriage. The harm at that point would be so severe that he does not think it will violate his values to disengage from the relationship by ending their marriage.

Keep in mind that someone else experiencing very similar marriage problems may have come to a completely different conclusion. This example is not meant to illustrate that there is one right thing to do in a situation that involves infidelity, but rather to show that the Decision Tree was able to help Stephen get clarity on his values, his desires, and his options. It helped him honestly examine the issues without either wishful thinking or knee-jerk defense mechanisms. It led him to pick a way forward that he felt was right for him in the moment. In later chapters, we will see how he handles his boundaries around this decision. Boundaries have really gotten the pop psychology treatment, so we will need a few chapters to establish what they really are and how they can help you in your relationships. The short of it is that boundaries are more than what we do or don't do; they are an internal knowing of where our responsibility ends and another person's responsibility begins. From this inner sense of boundaries flows our decisions on how we best proceed in each situation.

do you have a responsibility to stay together for the kids?

This is the number one concern a parent has when they consider whether to disengage from a relationship where they share children with their partner. Most of us have grown up on stories about how damaging it is for kids to come from a "broken home."

The decision to disengage from a partner when you have minor children can be incredibly difficult. In most situations, there is going to be some

distressing and destabilizing effects on children, at least temporarily.
As a parent, I understand the deep and primal drive to sacrifice anything to ensure that your children are happy and healthy. Most parents would jump in front of a bullet for their children. I'm not trying to change that.

But before you jump, I'd like to suggest that you ensure that getting in front of that bullet actually stops the bullet. If the bullet goes through you and hits your children anyway, now you have a child with a gunshot wound and a parent who can't help them.

Here is what I mean: Your child doesn't need a stable, peaceful, healthy *home*. What they need is a stable, peaceful, happy *parent*. This distinction is important.

Research shows that children who remain in high-conflict marriages actually have significantly more behavioral and mental health issues than children of parents who leave those marriages. When parents split up, regardless of whether the relationship was moderately happy or highly dysfunctional, the most important factor for children's emotional and social well-being is whether the parents engage in a high-conflict relationship with each other after the breakup.

So, if you are wondering whether you have a responsibility to stay together for the kids, ask yourself these three questions:

1. What impact does my current relationship have on my children?

2. What kind of environment might I be able to create for my children if I disengage from this relationship?

3. How would leaving this relationship affect my physical and emotional well-being and functioning? Are these things I can address while staying in the relationship or are they dependent on my leaving?

From here, you can start making the right decisions not only for the sake of your kids but for yourself.

questions for you:
assessing the depth of the relationship

Grab a pen and paper and fill in the blank scales below. Your answers and rankings are subjective. Don't worry about whether you are answering them "right" or "wrong." It's not a math formula but a way for you to see what you think and feel about the situation.

1. **What is the depth of the relationship?** Consider both the history of the relationship and the closeness you feel.

2. **What is the level of interdependence?** How much do you depend on each other? What commitments have you made to each other?

3. **What is the extent of any spiritual or cultural values that dictate your responsibilities to this person?**

4. **What is the severity of the harm?** How does their behavior affect you? How much damage does their behavior cause?

what next?

Whether we stay in a relationship or disengage, most of us want to feel we are acting with integrity. These questions are designed to help you determine how to do that. You've likely come to one of the following conclusions:

- You have met your responsibilities to this relationship and now you want to disengage.

  Give yourself permission to disengage from this relationship—you have done what you can. The next section will explore what disengaging means with boundaries so you can choose a path forward that feels right to you.

- You have ongoing responsibilities to this relationship, so at this time you will stay in it.

  Remember, this doesn't mean you do nothing. In fact, there might be a great many changes you need to make in the way you interact in this relationship. The section on staying with boundaries will explore what that may look like.

staying with boundaries and disengaging with values: what that looks like

The general categories of "stay" or "disengage" are nuanced. There are lots of ways to continue a relationship and lots of ways to disengage from one. Staying or leaving looks different in each relationship when implemented with boundaries, something we will explore in detail in part 3.

Here are several examples of how different people might stay in a relationship while implementing boundaries:

- Betty decides to remain married to her husband, who has alcohol use disorder, after he relapsed. *However*, she enacts boundaries to minimize the harmful impact of his addiction on herself and their small children: She and their children live separately from her husband, and he visits several times a week to eat dinner with the kids.

- Gloria decides to maintain a relationship with her parents, who do not accept her sexual identity and often pick fights with her about her partner. *However*, she enacts boundaries to protect herself and her partner. She doesn't invite her parents to her home. When she visits them, it's without her partner. When she visits her parents, she stays in a hotel to get frequent breaks if interactions get too negative.

- Darren decides to maintain his relationship with his oldest childhood friend, whose mental health issues make it hard for him to be there for Darren when Darren needs him. *However*, Darren enacts boundaries that protect himself from harm. This has involved lowering his expectations of the friendship. They catch up and hang out occasionally, but Darren knows to turn to other friends when he needs emotional support. The relationship is happier but more superficial.

- Mike and Shanel decide that it's no longer safe for their twenty-year-old son to visit them at home, but they still want to maintain a relationship with him. *However*, they enact boundaries around their interactions. They affirm that they will always answer the phone when he calls if he isn't aggressive, and they agree to meet him at a nearby restaurant to buy him a meal and spend time with him once a month.

Here are four examples of how disengaging while maintaining your values can look:

- Bethany decides to stop engaging with her father because he becomes verbally abusive when she visits him in his nursing home. Although she has chosen not to speak with him directly, she feels that it is still important to her values to oversee his care from a distance. She helps him pay for his nursing home and consults his nurses and doctors. Her husband visits him twice a month to make sure he is getting the level of care he needs.

- Carole decides to disengage from her ex-husband, who has lied about his employment and financial issues for years. She informs her ex that she is only willing to speak with him about their children.

- Kim decides to cut ties with her girlfriend after she cheated. Kim has consulted the Decision Tree and her values, and she feels that she wants no direct contact with her ex. She blocks her on social media to avoid running into her virtually. She asks their mutual friends to refrain from discussing her ex with her or sharing information about Kim with her ex.

- Ana decides that she wants to leave her husband after realizing that his constant name-calling and belittling is chronic mistreatment. However, Ana has no money, no family, and is concerned that he will become a safety threat if she tries to leave. Her plan for disengagement involves getting help from professionals and avoiding conflict for the time being. The process will take many months, possibly longer.

Disengaging is not always permanent. Bethany may decide to begin visiting her father again if his condition changes or she feels she can deal with his behavior after having a break. Carole may reconsider her boundaries if her ex-husband undergoes therapy to help with his financial issues and obsessive lying.

the takeaway:

The decisions made after reviewing the Decision Tree are not intended to be permanent. Instead, the Decision Tree offers a way to think about relationships that allows you to reassess when necessary.

how to compare your relationship with others, and why it's sometimes a good thing

I want what they have isn't a vice—it's a beacon.
Follow it (the right way).

Comparison is often said to be the thief of joy. The grass is always greener on the other side is a cliché for a reason—we often need to remind ourselves that the things we don't have sometimes appear shinier than the things we do have. As the mother of two preschool-aged girls, I can assure you that nothing makes an old boring toy look new than to have your sister start playing with it.

Tyler Perry put this in perspective in his movie *Why Did I Get Married?* In it, two husbands discuss the eighty-twenty rule: In any relationship, you'll get only 80 percent of what you need. When you find that other 20 percent in another person, you may mistakenly believe that you'll be happier, more fulfilled if you go after that person who has the 20 percent you feel you're missing. But the reality is that they took for granted the person who had much more to offer.

This is an important lesson to learn, but it can also be weaponized to keep people in relationships that aren't serving them because they're *okay enough.* Comparison may be a thief, but it can also be a wake-up call, causing you to realize that your standards are too low and the behavior being offered to you in a relationship is subpar.

I often think of the viral TikTok video of a woman, eight months pregnant, cleaning the house while her husband goofs off with their kids. "Sometimes I wish I had a husband who helped around the house more," she says in voice-over, "but then I realized that I need to be grateful that my kids have a 'fun dad.'"

Dear readers: This makes me want to scream. I can imagine that this woman complained about constantly cleaning to someone who responded by telling her to be more grateful for having a husband who is engaged at all. I would like to find that person and throw them into a volcano.

Millions of people are in relationships with fun dads who *also* clean their house. Millions of women have partners who recognize the toll pregnancy takes on a body and help ease that burden. If this woman is looking around and comparing her relationship to others and realizing she is getting the shit end of the deal, she is not being ungrateful. She is coming to the correct conclusion.

Some of us never had caring relationships modeled for us. We need to observe to figure out what is "healthy," because we don't know this intuitively. We don't want to fall into the eighty-twenty trap, later realizing we didn't appreciate the good things that we had because someone isn't perfect, but we also don't want to gaslight ourselves into overlooking real problems.

So how do we compare correctly?

I know a couple who are very physically affectionate in public. He is always kissing her and pulling her onto his lap. As someone who really enjoys physical affection, I feel sadness when I compare that aspect of their relationship to mine. My husband is not naturally a physically affectionate person.

Let's explore a great short exercise to use if you're confused about a relationship behavior before you even get to the Decision Tree.

questions for you:
comparing correctly

Grab a pen and paper or any recording device and answer the following questions.

1. **Ask yourself, *What is this behavior an example of?***
   This provides some generalizing perspective on what is occurring.
   In the case of the PDA couple, I would answer:
   Displays of affection and desire.

2. **Then ask yourself how important the behavior is to you.** You can even try to rate the importance on a scale of one to ten.
   For me, I would answer:
   It would be ten out of ten. A partnership without romantic affection is unacceptable to me, even if my partner is a good provider or a good father.

3. **Next, ask yourself, *What are examples of my partner showing affection and desire?***
   I would answer:
   He tells me I look beautiful; he pats the seat next to him affectionately when I walk by to ask me to be close to him; he writes me love notes, gives snuggles and hugs when I initiate them. The list would go on.

Contemplating these questions gives you the space and reflection to uncover what is absent and what you need. This simple practice showed me that what I saw in that other relationship was already present in mine, just in a different form. My husband's affectionate acts are not grand gestures of physicality—but they're genuine. And they work for me.

Let's look at a non-romantic example. Fantasy novelist Aparna Verma shared a story on TikTok of coming to terms with the way her father showed love when she self-published her debut novel. "I was thinking about how my immigrant father has a hard time showing his emotions to me," she said, "but when I self-published my book, he called all his friends to tell them to preorder it. He would go to the post office every day to ship out my books, made friends with the post office lady, and now he tells all his Uber customers that I'm a 'big-time author' when I've only started my career."

Aparna posted this story with a video of her father dressed up and walking into Barnes & Noble, clearly very proud to celebrate the publication of her book in stores.

Aparna may or may not still have issues with her father's inability to verbally express emotions, but what she's done is something deeply profound—she has seen her father. She *sees* how he loves her in his own way. It may not look like the love that her friends' fathers give them, but it is so clearly present.

information, not obligation

Asking yourself these questions when you find yourself comparing your relationships to others' enables you to gather information. In some cases, you may gain a new perspective, as I did when looking at the way my husband shows affection compared to how another person's husband does. In other cases, you may decide that regardless of whether a behavior is present in some form, it's simply a deal-breaker for you to not receive love or help or support in the way that you need. The next step would be to consult the Decision Tree.

The presence of some good things in a relationship does not justify hurtful things. You aren't obligated to stay in a harmful relationship just because the other person is doing their best, but it certainly is vital information to consider when deciding how you will proceed. After all, we've already learned how powerful it can be to gain a new, more accurate story about someone.

Let's revisit our pregnant friend from the TikTok video who was frustrated by her husband's refusal to clean. If she did this exercise, she may conclude one of three things:

1. She can ask herself what the act of cleaning is an example of. What does it represent to her?

   Partnership, she might answer, *and consideration for my well-being.*

2. She can ask herself how important cleaning is to their relationship.

   I won't speak for her, but from her TikTok posts, it seems that his refusal would be ranked high in importance since it seems to really bother her.

3. She can then step back and ask herself if there are other examples of partnership and consideration in their marriage relating to the home.

   Maybe her husband is a champ at managing homework and cooking dinner.

What then does she make of his refusal to engage in cleaning? Perhaps he finds cleaning hard and is desperately procrastinating on a task he loathes. Perhaps she feels the same way about cooking. This would be enlightening for how she understands this issue at hand and how to move forward.

On the other hand, maybe there really aren't many examples of partnership and consideration in their marriage. Maybe he shirks most duties outside of playing with the kids on the weekends. As a result of doing this exercise, she sits down and does some honest assessing of their marriage and concludes that this issue is a symptom of a serious underlying theme: He shows up only in the areas *he* cares about— and leaves all the tedious tasks to her.

Which of these scenarios means that she ought to leave her marriage? Which means that she ought to decide *Well, this is good enough*?

That's a trick question. The choice to stay or leave a marriage—or any relationship—is deeply intimate and nuanced. The world is rife with moralizing statements about which decision makes you weak or strong, empowered or a coward. I do not wish to presume to know what is best for this woman, or for you—and I believe oversimplified judgments are deeply harmful. The Decision Tree would help her begin to consider which decision is right for her.

Sometimes it's scary being honest when it comes to assessing relationships. You may feel that if you face the absolute truth about a situation you will "have to do something," and if you don't do that thing you will be judged, even if only by yourself. I'd like to relieve that anxiety. Assessing a relationship is a journey of gentle information seeking. This will take time. You are likely to change your mind several times. Your views of other people and their behavior may change several times. It's a process—a journey. And with an open mind, the destination now unknown will become clearer in time.

I won't judge you, whatever you eventually decide is best for you— I believe you.

the takeaway:

Comparison can be a useful tool when used as a way to understand your own relationship better and assess what is present and what is missing.

why the small moments matter

*Call me controversial, but I believe
it's reasonable to expect that the people
you are in a relationship with like you.*

My husband dances. Not professionally. Not at parties or events. Not when anyone else is around but me. Not to music. Never to music. It's a funny kind of dance where he moves his arms like waves and pumps his chest, bending his knees in a bounce and smiling wide. Picture an octopus.

He does it when he's happy, but the dance isn't just about expressing a good mood. It's not an involuntary happy dance or stim. Its sole purpose is to connect with me. And it has gotten the same responses from me for the past ten years: Either I join him, or I say, "Ohhh, he dances!" in a playfully serious tone. Sometimes this elicits "I do my dance!" back from him.

It's a moment of playfulness between two partners, like inside jokes I share with my friends. Perhaps you have moments such as these in your own relationships. These little requests for connection—what famous therapists and marriage researchers John and Julie Gottman call bids—are where one person engages and the other responds. They are the backbone of a relationship.

Bids can be huge events. Marriage proposals. Homecoming asks. A phone call where you squeak out, "Do you have time to talk?" between tears. But the bids that sustain a loving relationship long term are the small and subtle ones. Bids occur for all kinds of connection—between parent and child, friends, and lovers.

Sometimes it's reaching for someone's hand; sometimes it's rolling your eyes at the same person at the same time. Sometimes it's an inside joke, or a story about what you saw on the subway, or a silly little dance. It's an invitation to watch TV. It's drawing their attention to a sunset you find beautiful. These moments, when reciprocated, are the links in the chain of connection that make life so great.

If you're old enough to remember when Facebook was young, there used to be this poke feature. When you clicked the "poke" button on someone's profile, Facebook would send that person a notification that said, "So-and-so poked you." What did poking mean? Well, not really anything. It was just a way of saying "Hey there!" Think of bids like those early Facebook pokes. Little moments that say, "I see you! Let's connect!"

When my husband does his little dancey-dance bid, and I respond with dancing or being playful, I am doing what relationship experts call turning toward him. If I were to dismiss his bid by staring instead at my phone or acting annoyed, then that would be turning away from the bid. There is a third way to respond, turning against, where I actively belittle or undermine his bid by saying something like, "God, you look so stupid."

Ways to respond to bids:

- Turning toward—being attentive

- Turning away—being dismissive

- Turning against—being aggressive

You might guess that if I regularly responded to my husband's dancing by ignoring or dismissing it, then it would eventually erode the trust and affection we've built for each other. One study measured how frequently a select group of couples turned toward each other's bids during a weekend together and then followed up with each couple six years later. The researchers found that couples who were happiest six years later had turned toward each other's bids during that first weekend 87 percent of the time. The ones who broke up or were unhappy six years later only turned toward each other 33 percent of the time.

how to respond to bids without pretending

A couple of years ago, a video of a man referencing the study on bids went viral.

"When one partner says, 'Oh, look what a beautiful bird outside,' does the partner respond by saying something like, 'Wow, that is beautiful,' or do they blow their partner off and ignore the bird? It's a tiny moment, but that's what makes it important," he said. He ended the video with, "When the love of your life points out a bird, look at the fucking bird!"

This video got 14.7 million views. It spawned more than 274,000 shares and countless reposts. Every time I would see someone repost that video they always pasted the same text at the top: "Look at the fucking bird!" Some of the people who reposted had visible pain in their eyes—the pain of having or remembering a partner who couldn't be bothered to be interested in the things they were interested in.

And while I felt deeply for those individuals, I couldn't help feeling sorry for someone else as well. The people who don't like birds.

Let me explain. I don't want you to mistakenly believe that answering your partner's bids for connection in this instance must require *pretending* to be interested in birds.

If you take the moment to look at the bird, and you find yourself thinking, *Wow, cool bird*, then yes, saying "Wow, cool bird" to your partner is a lovely moment of connection. But if you could give two shits about birds, is looking at a bird and making a fake performance of enjoyment really a moment of connection?

You convey a *feeling* of connection to your partner if your acting is convincing enough, but you won't experience it as a moment of true connection. To have to constantly pretend you find something interesting that you find boring just to spare the feelings of others sounds lonely. That's the opposite of connection.

At the same time, I'm not suggesting that blowing off your partner or ignoring the bird is the best way to respond, either. Too much disregard and meanness get justified in the spirit of honesty for my taste. But surely there must be a better way to honor both people than to say we must choose between being hurtful or being fake.

I suggest that truly turning toward a person's bid for connection requires a response that is both caring and authentic.

I wish I could give you a specific formula for how to do this, but it's unique to each person. Bids are not the same for all couples. There are ways to incorporate your unique personalities and connection styles in your bids even if you struggle to connect and/or if you don't actually like the bid that's being offered.

I'll give an example from my own life.

As it so happens, I am into birds. I've spent countless hours in my backyard watching birds. I research the best bird feeders and the pros and cons of each seed type. I relocated where I work during the day, all but abandoning the upstairs office I made for myself, to work in front of the bay window in front of my feeders so the birds can dazzle me all day long. I downloaded an app and learned the names of every bird that came to my feeder, making observations on which seemed to be the bird bullies and which the underdogs (underbirds?). I observed which birds had a mate and which ones were on the hunt. I put in a birdbath and just as quickly removed it when I found a dead bird in it. Deciding the bird's death was a result of hitting the window, I researched the best decals to prevent future strikes. I waged a three-week war with the local squirrels, oiling up the feeder poles to make them too slippery to climb.

The pleasure I took in my backyard birds was almost as great as the pleasure I took in regaling Michael about my daily bird adventures.

Michael, however, is not into birds.

One day during a particularly impassioned retelling of the day's bird happenings, I watched as the old familiar smile, the suppressing of a full-out laugh, spread across his face.

I responded with "You don't care about this at all, do you?"

To which he teased me affectionately: "I love . . . that you love the birds."

Thus began a running joke between us about the birds.

"You watchin' your birds?" he'd ask with amusement when finding me at my bay window.

"If you were really a cultured man, you'd be into the birds," I'd remind him.

"So many bird things to tell you about when you get home," I text him when he's away.

And once, while I was outside hanging up a new feeder, he ran into the lawn and exclaimed with fake outrage, "No! I draw the line, KC. No more birds!"

"Birds are important, Michael!" I yelled back in mock chastisement.

"They are RATS WITH WINGS, KC," he yelled as I doubled over in laughter. "RATS. WITH. WINGS!"

This isn't to say every bird reference is met with a performance. If it's too early in the morning for Michael to feel playful, he might barely lift his head out of his coffee mug and give me a bored but authentic "Oh yeah." Which is fine with me—sufficient for my need for connection given how much joking we do about birds on a regular basis.

I can't prescribe my very specific dynamic with Michael as the way *you* need to respond to your partner's bids. What I hope you take from my example is simply that sometimes the enjoyment in a bid comes from the enjoyment you get witnessing your partner's enjoyment—not from your interest in the topic. It's delighting in another person's delight.

You do not need to love everything your partner or friend or child loves. And your partner, friend, or child does not need to enjoy the things you love. But you deserve to have a relationship in which the other person *sees you in the things you love*.

are bids the cure or just the symptom?

Since couples who are unhappy or break up frequently turn away from bids, whereas couples who stay together frequently answer bids, it's easy for relationship therapists to interpret this as *Okay, folks, we need to learn to get better at bids!*

Is the conclusion that bids keep people happy? Or is it more accurate to conclude that people who enjoy each other's presence are happier?

They don't just enjoy what they do for each other or what they provide. Rather they enjoy the little moments. They delight in what the other delights in. It makes them happy to see the other person happy.

I'm not sure enjoying your partner is a skill that can be taught. You either like your partner or you don't.

Now if you do like your partner but due to barriers of culture, communication, neurotype, or trauma (to name a few), you struggle to express your love for them in a way that they can feel and vice versa, then yes, the skill of learning to recognize and turning authentically into someone else's bids is something that can be learned and developed. The key here is that there is a difference between *We feel affection and enjoyment for each other, but we struggle to connect in a meaningful way* and *We struggle to feel affection and enjoyment of each other*.

Learning to get better at bids can only
help you express an affection you already feel.
Getting good at turning into bids
does not create affection or enjoyment.

In many relationships, couples who love each other can become disconnected. Even though they love each other, getting back to a dynamic where they *enjoy* each other can be difficult because trust has been so broken or life has been so hard. In these cases, taking time to intentionally turn into each other's bids can help to restore trust and affection. Again, turning in doesn't have to mean pretending, but it does mean reconceptualizing your partner's actions as attention and outreach and learning to appreciate their desire to connect with you. Can you find pleasure in their pleasure, or affection in their desire to share something with you? If not, do you want to? Are you willing to work toward getting back to that place? If you both do, sally forth. I've seen more than one couple come back from the brink of hating each other. But I must warn you: I have never seen a couple recover where only one person is willing to fight. And you can't make someone fight.

the takeaway:

The backbone of a connected relationship is the small-moment acts of connection where one person acknowledges the other as a way of signaling: I see you. And I like what I see.

making decisions with your head and your heart

Passion and wisdom can coexist, if you ask the right questions.

I spent my early twenties in an evangelical church that encouraged the young adult congregants to marry early and quickly. Marriage was a holy endeavor that gave you a special status in the church. There was also an emphasis on gender roles, where men were expected to be leaders and providers and women were expected to act as modest caretakers. Marriage enabled emotional and physical intimacy—so marrying early and quickly was incentivized on multiple levels. All this culminated in a rush to find the right partner (referred to by Christians in college as getting a "ring by spring").

In this cultural pressure cooker, dating was more like going on job interviews. Each of us had a Good Church Boy/Girl checklist, a list of attributes necessary in a mate. The first time you found someone who seemed qualified enough (and you were attracted to them), you scooped them up and ran down to the altar.

But this eagerness to pair up with the first person who met the criteria had a dark side. With my addiction history, I joined the recovery ministry at my church, which offered support groups for various struggles, including marital issues. During these sessions, I was continually surprised by the number of couples who didn't seem to *like* each other. I don't mean they felt animosity toward each other, either; rather, the years had stripped away the initial excitement about marriage and many found themselves to be mere business partners. It was strange to see young newlyweds celebrated and beaming with pride every Sunday in the sanctuary and then encounter middle-aged men and women who seemed to have nothing in common anymore trying to salvage relationships every Thursday in the recovery groups. It seemed as though many of them had mistaken the initial excitement of having found a spouse with the happiness of loving someone because you are delighted by who they are.

The practice of "résumé dating," where you seek a checklist of accomplishments or attributes that measure what someone can *do* for you in a relationship, doesn't live only in conservative or religious communities. Being enamored with *the idea* of having a partner shows up in podcasts and social media—where "high-value men" teach other men to seek out submissive women to cook and clean, and women teach other women how to snag a rich man for a transactional relationship. It lives on, too, in far less repulsive ways, in those of us who are attracted to people based primarily in what they can provide for us—social status, economic stability, sexual satisfaction, or self-esteem.

Sure, some are forthright about marrying for money or beauty. And some of these people might genuinely be happy with their choices. But for the rest of us, who want emotional connection and friendship in our romantic relationships, we may struggle long term if this checklist mentality dominates our search for connection.

This kind of status seeking is a developmentally appropriate motivation for new relationships during puberty. Preteens and teenagers don't have much of a distinctive identity formed yet, or at least not one they are confident enough to explore, so it makes sense that they base relationships around social hierarchies.

But many of us get stuck there. Whether we never felt safe enough to develop or explore our own identity or struggled to heal from trauma that disrupted the development of a healthy self-concept, many of us are socially and emotionally arrested in this adolescent stage of self-consciousness. We never learned to value or enjoy people for their unique identities on their own terms. We continue, even into adulthood, to make decisions based on how cool or sexy someone is to the rest of the world and what it will mean to our social status to be seen with them, or to our self-esteem if we are wanted by them.

Perhaps I would have been trapped in this adolescent stage of relationships had I not met my first boyfriend when I was sixteen. Let's call him Perry. Although the relationship didn't last long, it was the kind of relationship that cracks open the sky.

I had had romantic and sexual experiences before this relationship, but they were fundamentally different. I enjoyed these prior relationships because being wanted by boys felt good. I still assessed romantic and sexual relationships through the lens of social capital.

But Perry was different. For the first time, I got to know a boy for who he really was—what he loved, what made him laugh, what he felt passionate about and was gifted in. I saw him as a truly unique human, and I felt more like myself than I had ever before. We talked about everything. Explored every topic. He was equally as enchanted with me as I was with him. And that love seeped into my soul and imprinted itself in my DNA and changed something about me.

Then, we were both sent away to teen rehabs.

After nearly two years in rehab, we briefly reunited, but life was complicated. I was newly sober, and we had grown into different people. Although our first love as teenagers was moving and real, I knew in my heart that the people we had become could not create a meaningful life together. It would have been unloving of me to try to resurrect our teenage selves. They didn't exist anymore. So I left them in the past, where they are happy.

The greatest gift the relationship with Perry gave me was the knowledge that true connection was possible. Trouble was, I didn't believe I'd ever find it again.

Then, to my surprise, Michael.

In a world dominated by "let's hang out," Michael had refreshing clarity. I had experienced one too many "situationships" where I had misread the tone of the relationships or, even worse, where the other person was purposefully using the lack of clarity to take from me without being on the hook to give anything back. But from the beginning, Michael, who was twenty-three when we met, had the courage and confidence to be clear about his desires and intentions from the beginning of the relationship.

In just a few weeks, I fell deeply in love. If my teenage boyfriend was a lightning storm, Michael was the ocean. His entry into my life was simultaneously a passionate tempest and a calm, safe sea stretching out to the horizon—beautiful and otherworldly. All I wanted was to be in his presence, see the world through his eyes, to hear him laugh. If I lived a thousand lives, I would find him in every one.

Reader, I was in CONFLICT.

These feelings slammed up against my Good Church Boy checklist. While we shared the same faith, which I knew I wanted in a partner, he didn't subscribe to my church's ideas about gendered roles, church authority, or premarital sex. Michael was also a former addict, but one who had only two years sober to my ten. This terrified me. I had seen too many people relapse. My pastor told me he liked Michael fine, but that he was a rebel, someone I needed to be weary of.

I wanted sky-splitting, ocean-deep love and friendship, and here it was, but I wasn't quite sure that it was safe to take such a leap without those checklist items ticked off. For every loveless couple who married using the checklist, there were also those who followed their heart, who became blinded by love and passion, and fell into untenable situations with someone who wasn't good for them.

I needed a way to assess this relationship that took into account my head *and* my heart. I was not about to settle for a good-on-paper partner without that sky-splitting attraction and joy. But I also wanted to make wise decisions. So, I developed a new checklist:

questions for you:
assessing a relationship for passion and wisdom

So you've met someone you are attracted to. The seeds of passion are there: You feel drawn to be around them and learn more about them; you feel attractive and interesting in their presence; the idea of doing things together excites you, and you can't wait to see them again; you could see yourself caring about this person.

Grab a pen and paper or a recording device of some sort and answer the following questions to assess whether this potential relationship is a good blend of passion *and* wisdom.

1. **Do you share the same essential expectations for a future relationship?**

   1. Are you looking for a casual friendship/dating partner, long-term, or even lifelong friend or partner?

   2. Do you want to have fun and live separate lives right now but eventually cohabitate, marry, and have kids?

   3. Are you a monogamist, or do you want to explore polyamory or open relationships?

2. **Does the person you're attracted to have a drive to live a meaningful life? What does a meaningful life mean to you? What does it mean to them?**

1. Do you want someone who participates in social justice causes?

2. Is it important for them to have spiritual commitments?

3. Is political activism or a particular political leaning important to you?

3. How do they take initiative and show ambition toward their goals—career or otherwise?

4. How do they take initiative and show ambition toward building a relationship with you?

5. Do they show respect for their commitments?

6. Do they treat you with dignity and respect even when they are angry?

7. How do they talk about and treat those who are weaker, more vulnerable, or have less power?

8. Do they express sympathy to people who cannot do anything for them?

9. Do they handle being wrong in ways you admire?

When I answered these questions for myself all those years ago, I felt more confident that the earth-shattering love was on the right track.

- ☑ Michael wanted what I wanted: long-term monogamous love and a family.

- ☑ Yes, he had only two years of sobriety—but I observed how dedicated he was to it.

- ☑ Yes, he was broke, but so was I. Yet I admired his ambition and work ethic. When he needed money to take me on dates, he got a tutoring gig on the side. He saved up money for a couch from the Salvation Army so we had somewhere to sit in his apartment. He got a third job at Sherwin-Williams so he could save money for an engagement ring. I didn't know where either of our careers might take us, but I was willing to live in a cardboard box if it meant being his partner.

- ☑ He may have been "resistant to authority" by church standards, but I saw him seek out mentors and ask for advice many times.

- ☑ He was emotionally mature. I saw him admit when he was wrong and do the right thing even when it was difficult.

Ten years have passed, and I'm still grateful that I changed my checklist to fit my unique perspective—and in doing so, changed the course of my life.

the pitfall of potential

While some struggle with needing potential partners to meet an unreasonable checklist of qualities and accomplishments, others may have the opposite problem. They see potential everywhere. How many people have stayed in a relationship for far too long waiting for their partner to change and become the person they want them to be?

If only they fixed their anger problem . . .

If only they stopped drinking . . .

If only they got a job and really applied themselves . . .

If only they focused on settling down . . .

If only they left the party life behind . . .

If only they went to therapy . . .

Then they would be a great partner!

I believe potential only matters when you are looking at someone who has had a lack of opportunities, not someone who is demonstrating a lack of effort or integrity. One is about guessing trajectory based on current behavior, the other is about hoping for a sudden change in trajectory despite there being no evidence for it.

It's about how people act, not necessarily the context that surrounds them at this particular point in their journey. For example, having no money in the bank tells you nothing about someone's ambition, work ethic, or responsibility. They might be a person who isn't willing to work hard and spends money frivolously, or they might be someone who quit college to care for the crushing medical costs of their sibling's illness.

the takeaway:

When it comes to picking a romantic partner, don't settle for good-on-paper if you feel no attraction or joy. When you do find someone who sparks that passion, amend your checklist to focus on your values and goals, instead of specific traits.

part three

how to use boundaries to have better relationships

boundaries are the opposite of control

Why Jonah Hill is a dick and other thoughts on boundaries.

The Decision Tree helped you discover whether staying in or disengaging from a particular relationship is right for you. Now, we will talk about *how* to stay or disengage—with boundaries. Every piece of sound advice about staying, leaving, or healing relationships involves working with boundaries.

Unfortunately, boundaries are a misapplied concept in pop-psychology circles. To start, let's define exactly what boundaries are—and what they aren't. Boundaries are not quippy one-liners where you tell someone to stop abusing you or else. They're also not consequences conjured up to get someone to change their behavior as though they're a child. My goal is to give you a new way to think about boundaries that *has nothing to do with controlling how someone else behaves*.

In the summer of 2023, actor Jonah Hill came under fire when his ex-girlfriend, surfer and law student Sarah Brady, posted screenshots of Jonah's texts, outlining his relationship "boundaries."

Despite Jonah saying that he used "boundaries," Sarah rightly called out his behavior as controlling and emotionally abusive. Jonah's behavior illustrates something I see as a therapist all the time: The belief that slapping therapeutic labels (such as "boundaries") on problematic and controlling behavior magically makes it appropriate behavior. Jonah had been public in an earlier documentary about the years spent in therapy and his mental health journey, so we know he is well-versed in the language of this world.

If Jonah had said, "It bothers me when you do these things," and left room for the possibility that some of his discomfort may be coming from the activation of his own sensitivities, then there would have been an opportunity for an open dialogue between two people who are peers.

Instead, Jonah used therapy-speak to present himself and his concerns as superior. He implied that she was not able to trust herself to know what was and wasn't healthy behavior—but he knew. He was the healthy, enlightened one and she was the unhealthy, immature one. This enacted an imbalanced power dynamic in which Jonah loved Sarah enough to "help" her even though she was far beneath him.

His list was bizarre. While it may be reasonable to feel upset if you think your partner does not have appropriate boundaries with other men, his concerns were mostly a list of perfectly normal behaviors such as surfing with male friends, modeling, and appearing in pictures in a swimsuit. While every person has a right to their opinion of what is and isn't appropriate behavior, Sarah pointed out to Jonah in subsequent texts that he knew all these things about her before they started dating. After all, she was a surfing instructor and a model when he chose to date her!

Regardless of the language he used, it's clear that the whole purpose of his text was to manipulate Sarah into behaving in a way that soothed his insecurities.

Sarah was right. When someone else tries to control who you see, how you dress, or where you work, it's a red flag. Someone making you feel like they are doing you a favor by being with you and leading you to think you cannot trust your own version of reality is a hallmark of abusive relationships.

Boundaries are the opposite of control. This coercion emerges from Jonah's sensitivities, which are inflaming his defense mechanisms. To understand why this is happening, he would have to start investigating. But that would take effort and real vulnerability—which he didn't seem to want to do—so he fell back on control tactics.

Everything in this text message shows us that Jonah was using the language of boundaries without having done the internal work of boundaries.

Boundaries aren't about what you say or do—real boundaries are internal.

If Jonah had real boundaries, he would not have sent those texts. He would have explored why his insecurities were triggered, taken responsibility for them, and communicated vulnerably with Sarah. He would have faced his real emotions instead of hiding behind the comfort of moral superiority. He would have ended a relationship that he felt wasn't right for him without the need to moralize and control. He certainly would not begin a relationship with someone thinking he could change them.

the internal work of boundaries

Jonah misunderstands boundaries—and he's in good company. The way boundaries have filtered down from pop psychology leaves many people confused. People think boundaries begin with a script on how to speak to people, a list of acceptable behaviors, and how to enact consequences when someone crosses your "boundary." With this misunderstanding of boundaries, any unreasonable request can become a boundary with the right therapy-speak.

The problem is that we are defining boundaries all wrong. Real boundaries aren't about what you say or do—they are internal. They provide a sense of where I end and you begin—what's my responsibility and what's not. Internal boundaries give us the ability to:

- Adopt a radical sense of agency over our own emotions and behavior.

- Recognize when the behavior and emotions of others are not our responsibility.

- Communicate to others in a way that is authentic while honoring the differences in relationships and contexts.

- Distinguish between what is our fault and what is our responsibility.

- Balance care of self and care for others.

- Balance outside input and intuition.

> *Having boundaries is about having a correct sense of self.*

If we think of a boundary as defining where you and I begin and end, then we can picture a line that separates us from another person. Our side of the line contains the things we have agency over and are responsible for. On their side of the line are the things we do not have agency over and are not our responsibility.

WHAT iS MY RESPONSIBILITY...

MY THOUGHTS
MY FEELINGS
MY BODY
MY BELIEFS
MY DECISIONS
MY BEHAVIOR
MY REACTIONS
MY VALUES
MY WORLDVIEW
MY RELIGION
MY MORALS
MY UNDERSTANDING
MY MENTAL HEALTH
MY UNDERSTANDING OF
   MY OBLIGATIONS
THE CONSEQUENCES OF
   MY ACTIONS

A BOUNDARY iS WHERE I END
AND YOU BEGIN.

THEIR THOUGHTS
THEIR FEELINGS
THEIR BODY
THEIR BELIEFS
THEIR DECISIONS
THEIR BEHAVIOR
THEIR REACTIONS
THEIR VALUES
THEIR WORLDVIEW
THEIR RELIGION
THEIR MORALS
THEIR UNDERSTANDING
THEIR MENTAL HEALTH
THEIR UNDERSTANDING OF
    THEIR OBLIGATIONS
THE CONSEQUENCES OF
    THEIR ACTIONS

boundaries aren't about the other person.

I'll go even further: Setting a boundary with another person isn't possible.

Let's say your sister constantly belittles other people behind their back about their weight in a way that you feel is a veiled commentary on *your* weight.

You might think you're setting a boundary when you say to her, "Don't make comments about other people's weight in my presence." But the reality is that you're just making a request. You are just asking her to do something that you'd like her to do. Do I think it's a reasonable request? Absolutely. But the reasonableness of a request doesn't magically make an unreasonable person honor it—even if you call it a boundary.

What if your sister refuses to honor your request? Some therapists would say that a boundary only exists if there are key consequences to crossing it. This response exasperates me. Are you really expected to give consequences to a fully grown adult in order to get them to treat you with respect? And what do you do if she continues to comment on weight? Threaten with another consequence? A more convincing one? A more painful one? Cut her off all together? What if she's willing to withstand your lack of relationship longer than you are? What if you rely on her for childcare and can't afford to cut her off? Now you're back in your therapist's office complaining about your sister's refusal to respect your boundaries. You're still the reactive one. You're still the powerless one. Where do you go from here?

Having boundaries means you can mentally map out what's your responsibility and what's not. On your side of the line are your needs, values, decisions, and body. Your responsibility to stand up for yourself is on your side. What your sister thinks or feels about your request or your feelings are not your responsibility or in your control.

The boundary here is showing up authentically in a relationship where you honor your feelings, speak your needs, and stand up for yourself if you want to *and you do not take responsibility for the feelings your sister has about it*.

Boundaries don't just tell us when to disengage from conversations, they also inform us when to speak up. If you're feeling afraid to speak up when your sister comments on your weight, it's usually because you're afraid of her reaction. Now, in situations where your safety might be at risk, not speaking up is probably best. But most of the time it's the emotional discomfort that you are avoiding.

The possibility of your sister becoming angry or sad distresses you. You might feel dysregulated by her disapproval or shame if she acts like you have hurt her. Perhaps she will be condescending and you will feel stupid, which is a key sensitivity for many people. This recalls that fight, flight, or freeze mode: even if there isn't a *physical* threat, our bodies register emotional threats as if we are in danger.

Let's say you decide that voicing your hurt over your sister's words is important to your sense of justice and self. Then say something. And ask her to stop. But if you feel that you'd rather keep yourself regulated emotionally and refrain from engaging in further conversation that might dysregulate you, then that is totally fine, too. The point is that you're taking action based on the decision to help yourself, not to control her, or change her, or because you are too afraid to be in the presence of her feelings. That's being boundaried.

When your brain registers the emotional reactions of others as a threat, you must do your own work of emotional regulation so that you can tolerate how it feels to be in the presence of someone else's raw feelings without trying to step over that boundary and fix it for them.

The request is not the boundary—standing up for yourself is.

HAVING BOUNDARIES IS NOT ABOUT GIVING SOMEONE CONSEQUENCES IF THEY DON'T HONOR YOUR REQUESTS. IT'S ABOUT SHOWING UP FOR YOURSELF AND BEING AUTHENTIC IN YOUR RELATIONSHIPS.

Whether your sister honors your request, you are still boundaried. You're clear that your sister's decision is her choice and it reflects her, not you. You won't be diminished in any way by her acceptance of your request (or refusal).

Here I want to clarify the idea of consequences. Consequences aren't a part of boundaries, but you can, and do, make decisions based on behavior. That is why the Decision Tree is not a one-time process but an ongoing assessment. The Decision Tree involves assessing how a person responds when you tell them their behavior is hurtful, and having that conversation involves boundaries. Perhaps after several instances of your sister refusing to change her behavior you decide you need to disengage. Remember, disengaging doesn't have to mean ending. It simply means making changes that add protection from their behavior in the form of emotional or physical distance. You may change how often or how vulnerably you engage with your sister, not because you're proving a point *to her*, but because you are genuinely protecting yourself *from her*.

Not all boundaries have to have a big behavioral follow-through. In fact, not all of them can. If you live with your sister or depend on her for support, you may not have the option to disengage entirely—or you may simply not want to. Maybe you decide that the best way to show up for yourself is that every time she mentions something negative about body image, you use the same words to reinstate your discomfort. Maybe you decide that from now on, you refuse to laugh it off and calmly state, "What a critical thing to say about someone."

Part of enacting this kind of a boundary is to refuse to take on the burden of the awkwardness, tension, or embarrassment of *her behavior* any longer. I call this return to sender. Maybe she now feels awkward or uneasy. Maybe she is angry that you keep bringing it up. This isn't in your control. But in addressing your feelings, you've refused to take on those feelings for the both of you. In this way, you remain engaged in a relationship with her in a boundaried way.

You are responsible for yourself. This is another powerful aspect of having boundaries—holding yourself accountable no matter how the other person may feel about it.

the takeaway:

Boundaries, when correctly applied, help you show up authentically in your relationships without taking responsibility for the resulting behavior or feelings of the other person.

boundaries mean being responsible

Long story short: Anyone who says "No one can make you feel anything" after acting like an ass, sucks and does not know what boundaries are.

When I say you are not responsible for the emotions and reactions of others, you may have breathed a sigh of relief. The idea that you do not have to go around managing the emotions of other people was welcome news. But you may have had an entirely different reaction, one of pain and grief as you recollect the cruelty and disrespect people in your life have justified by claiming they "aren't responsible for your feelings."

Make no mistake, not being responsible for other people's feelings does not mean you aren't responsible for your *behavior*. You are not responsible for other people's reactions, but you do have responsibilities to them.

Shirking accountability for hurtful or inconsiderate behavior and telling someone else how they must feel about it is a lack of boundaries. People get to feel however they feel about your behavior—and you don't get to control that. Having boundaries just means that someone else's feelings about your behavior is not the only factor that determines what you believe about yourself and what you choose to do next.

I HAVE A RESPONSIBILITY
 TO OTHERS TO ...

BE HONEST
SHOW EMPATHY
KEEP MY WORD
CONSIDER THEIR FEELINGS
CONSIDER FEEDBACK
CONFRONT
LEVEL WITH
LISTEN
BE AUTHENTIC
BE VULNERABLE

I DO HAVE RESPONSIBILITIES
 TO OTHERS.

THEIR THOUGHTS
THEIR FEELINGS
THEIR BODY
THEIR BELIEFS
THEIR DECISIONS
THEIR BEHAVIOR
THEIR REACTIONS
THEIR VALUES
THEIR WORLDVIEW
THEIR RELIGION
THEIR MORALS
THEIR UNDERSTANDING
THEIR MENTAL HEALTH
THEIR UNDERSTANDING OF
        THEIR OBLIGATIONS
THE CONSEQUENCES OF
        THEIR ACTIONS

Having boundaries means you listen, consider other people's feelings, try to understand the impact your behavior has on them, and then incorporate that into your decision-making process about your responsibilities to other people.

Let's say your mother wants to attend the birth of her grandchild, but your partner, the person giving birth, doesn't want her there. You feel conflicted. Your mom expressed a real desire to be there when the baby enters the world, and you don't want to hurt her feelings. But you know that it's important for your partner to feel backed up and as boundaried as possible during this momentous time.

Implementing boundaries in this situation is easier when you understand that your responsibility to your mother is different from your responsibility to your partner, with whom you are having a child. The good news is that you can uphold your responsibility to both people at the same time. You can tell your mother that while you appreciate her excitement, you will not be having her in the delivery room, but you would be delighted to see her after the baby is born.

In this case, you have met your responsibility to your partner by supporting their decision about who they want in the delivery room, and you have met your responsibility to your mother by communicating with kindness and honesty. You have no control over how your mother will take the news and it's not your responsibility to manage her reaction or make her understand your decision.

One of the greatest challenges with drawing boundaries is becoming comfortable with being misunderstood. When you go round and round with someone, getting sucked into trying to make them understand your motives and agree with your decision, you are crossing that boundary—across the line that separates you from them—by trying to control things you can't, which, in this case, is another person's emotions and perspectives.

Just allowing that another person can have a different reality than yours is one of the most boundaried things you can do.

If you chose to protect your mother's feelings (which are not your responsibility) at the expense of supporting your partner's decisions about how they wish to experience such an intimate and vulnerable event (which is your responsibility), then you did not make a boundaried decision. This decision would have been an example of people-pleasing behavior, something we will explore later in this chapter.

my hierarchy of responsibility

I believe we have a responsibility to all people to respect their human dignity. This doesn't mean being nice or even kind to everyone. It means refraining from acting in a way that maliciously pursues the suffering or degradation of another person.

Beyond that, responsibilities are going to look different in every relationship. This is true even in close relationships. When we are clear on what is and is not our responsibility, it's much easier to determine how to proceed in a way that's right for you and honors all the nuances.

Notice I said people do not have the right to *pursue* the suffering of another, rather than saying people do not have the right to cause suffering. Ethicist Eleanor Rushton makes this distinction between "causing" and "pursuing" suffering to distinguish between a situation where someone else's pain is the incidental outcome of a choice I have the right to make versus a situation where the purpose of my behavior is solely for the sake of causing pain. There may be instances where I acted ethically and still *caused* someone to suffer, such as breaking up with a partner who is now heartbroken, or fighting off an attacker who is hurt in the process and now in the ICU. That is very different from the intentional and malicious *pursuit* of someone else's suffering, such as cyberbullying someone because I don't like them, pretending to ask someone on a date just to stand them up and mock them, or taking naked pictures from someone only to turn around and post them on the internet to humiliate them. This distinction is important for being a boundaried person.

Our responsibilities in safe relationships may also include, depending on the context, a responsibility to:

- Be honest.

- Show empathy.

- Keep your word.

- Consider the feelings of others.

- Consider feedback.

- Confront harmful behavior.

- Consider the impact your behavior will have on others.

- Listen.

- Be authentic.

In close relationships that are safe, such as those with a good friend or longtime partner, there's also a responsibility to:

- Be vulnerable, because vulnerability is an essential part of honesty and authenticity.

- Carefully consider requests for emotional or practical support.

We cannot be everything to everyone, or even to everyone we are close to. Except for minor children, there are few relationships in which we have a wholesale responsibility to provide for the emotional or practical needs of someone else. However, part of belonging to an interdependent community means there may be many relationships in which you have a responsibility to at least carefully consider helping someone with a practical need. For example, it's not my responsibility to drive my friend to the airport. But in relationships and communities where I desire to create interdependence, I do have a responsibility to carefully consider how and when I might answer requests for support. How and when you offer practical support will depend on your abilities, resources, preferences, and boundaries within each relationship. My point here is only that we do have a responsibility to examine the big picture of whether we are doing our part to exist within interdependent relationships. It simply isn't true to claim we "don't owe anyone anything."

Keep in mind you do not need to uphold any part of the aforementioned list to anyone who acts in an abusive manner, no matter how close you are to them, and the responsibility to be vulnerable is to the few, not to the many. You do not owe vulnerability to, for example, your boss, a police officer, or a person you just met.

Let's look at varying responsibilities in two similar contexts.

In the first case, you lie to your occupational therapist about why you are switching therapists because you don't feel like having an uncomfortable conversation. In the second case, you lie to your occupational therapist about doing your exercise homework because you are afraid they will judge you. Technically both are "managing the reactions of other people."

But let's look deeper. In the first case, your decision about whether or not to tell the truth has no bearing on you or your occupational therapist—you don't owe them a critique of their services or an explanation of why you are leaving. Dogmatically forcing yourself to never tell a lie in situations like this is probably more about your own perfectionism than anything truly noble.

But lying about your exercise homework? That's a different story, because telling the truth or not can make the difference in getting the health care you need. The risk of being honest and vulnerable is worth the threat of being shamed, but you'll need to have solid boundaries to be comfortable taking such a risk. In the best-case scenario, you face your fear, and the occupational therapist kindly helps you create a more sustainable plan, causing your health and quality of life to improve. In the worst case, they're a Judgy McJudgerson who tells you you're lazy, in which case you'll have boundaries to know that judgment is a reflection on them and not you, and the emotional regulation skills to manage how shitty it felt to hear them say it. Then you can switch therapists and lie to them about why!

That being said, if you are looking to practice your emotional regulation skills and boundaries in small and safe ways, go ahead and tell that occupational therapist you are switching because you don't think they are a good fit for you. It's a small way to practice a big ability.

the takeaway:

You aren't responsible for other people, but you do have responsibilities to them.

people-pleasing and other overfunctioning behavior

As my mentor once said after I told her I struggled with people-pleasing, "Honey, look around. Ain't nobody pleased."

If you are a people pleaser, it means you deal with conflict by making yourself small. Maybe you've done this for years—cutting off parts of yourself and swallowing your own discomfort to make other people feel comfortable and maintain the peace. Maybe you don't even know what you really like or what you really think. You've always just put other people first.

Or have you?

Most people are shocked to realize that people-pleasing isn't about other people's comfort—it's about your own. It's about your sense of self being so determined by the opinions and feelings of others that you must manage those things by contorting yourself around the needs of others.

Here are some ways people-pleasing manifests.

- You say yes when you mean no and vice versa.

- You don't speak up for yourself.

- You don't express your opinions.

- You take on too much responsibility.

- You change your personality or appearance to fit what you think people want.

- You sugarcoat the truth to spare people's feelings.

- You feel you have a responsibility to diffuse people's anger.

- You feel you have a responsibility to cheer people up anytime they are upset.

- You give more emotionally or physically than you can afford to.

- You ignore problems in relationships.

I don't say this from a place of judgment but from a place of experience. Healing from people-pleasing means that you stop being controlled by other people's feelings and opinions. But you can't do that unless you realize that managing the feelings of others has always been a way to manage your own. You are depending on others' approval as an emotional regulation tool. When someone's anger, displeasure, or frustration triggers your fight or flight, you feel panic and fear. Perhaps you have some inaccurate beliefs about what it will mean if people do not like you—that you will be rejected or alienated. These thoughts and emotions are painful—and sometimes just the possibility that someone may be displeased with you can kick off your threat system.

If managing people is how you manage your emotions, identity, and well-being, you need to recognize that it's not your job to rescue others from feelings of distress. Instead, you need to practice the emotional regulation necessary to deal with your interpersonal fears and discomfort. These are the keys to becoming more boundaried so you can stop perpetually pleasing people and start authentically loving people.

note

It's important to distinguish between people-pleasing and pacifying an abusive person or system to ensure your own safety. People-pleasing behavior does not refer to choices you make to protect your physical or emotional safety, such as acquiescing to a police officer who is being aggressive, being polite to a pushy date you are alone with, or ignoring an insult from your abusive father. People-pleasing concerns the struggle you face in the effort to hang on to yourself in the face of someone else's normal and appropriate feelings.

overfunctioning in relationships

Constantly putting the needs of others before your own has often been referred to as codependency. But as I mentioned in the introduction, I do not like to use the term "codependency." I dislike that it's vaguely defined, that it often pathologizes normal emotional needs, that there is a stigma of shame attached to it, and that it's often used to describe an identity rather than a behavior.

Yet the feelings and experiences of people who identify with the term are valid. So how do we talk about the struggle to balance your needs and those of others in a more helpful way?

I think it is much more helpful to think about boundary mistakes, such as people-pleasing, as overfunctioning. Someone who overfunctions in relationships is constantly reaching over that boundary line to take responsibility for things that are not their responsibility.

boundary mistake

Every fall, after dropping their kids off for their first semester of college, so-called helicopter parents take to Facebook groups for parents of incoming first-year students and gift us with some of the best (and funniest) examples of what overfunctioning can look like.

"Does anyone know of a type of phone that can set off an alarm on someone else's phone?" one parent asked in a Facebook post. "[My son] has such a hard time waking up, I'm afraid he will miss class so I'm looking for something where I can wake him remotely (he sleeps through the phone ringing)."

Now, I'm not suggesting that a parent's responsibilities to their child end the moment they turn eighteen.

But I think most of us can agree that when an eighteen-year-old is attending college, it's no longer their parents' responsibility to wake them up in the morning. I would argue that it's the parents' responsibility **not** to wake your child up every morning so they can learn to wake up themselves. This is why overfunctioning is so unfortunate. The behavior often contributes to the other person never getting the opportunity to learn a new responsibility—thus becoming someone who **underfunctions**.

It's about understanding there is a difference between your responsibility to support your college-aged child and the belief that you are responsible for managing that adult child's behavior.

Whereas a person who overfunctions crosses their boundary line, someone who is underfunctioning consistently avoids their own responsibilities—tangible responsibilities, like financial obligations or contributing to housework, and emotional responsibilities, like controlling their own reactions and behavior.

Sometimes a person overfunctions in reaction to someone who first underfunctions. A spouse who exhausts themselves carrying more than their fair share of the family labor is often directly responding to a partner who refuses to lift a finger. What are they to do? They need clean clothes and a sanitary home, especially when children are involved, so they continue overfunctioning.

Enabling is a type of overfunctioning where you usurp responsibilities because you are afraid of letting the other person experience the consequences of their destructive behavior. I saw this constantly when working in rehabs. Families, terrified for their loved ones, mistakenly believed that they were helping when they paid their loved one's bills, hired expensive lawyers to keep them out of legal trouble, bought them new cars when the old one was wrecked, or lied to employers to cover up behavior. But this enabling behavior did little to truly help the person tackle their addiction. Instead, it kept families locked in a vicious cycle, where their own well-being was sacrificed in the name of managing the chaos caused by another person, who is never really helped. After a few years of this behavior, no one in the family is well.

As you can see, overfunctioning is much more than being considerate or trying to help someone out, it's when we insist on managing someone else's responsibilities *out of fear, guilt, control, or misplaced obligation*. It is a common relationship dynamic. Getting out of this dynamic takes strong boundaries.

Let's look at an example:

underfunctioning in a relationship

Your friend asks to borrow money for rent because he's been hit with a few unexpected medical bills and is late on rent. You might choose to help him out if you can. *We're all human*, you tell yourself. Someone once helped you out of a tight financial spot and feel you want to pay it forward. That's great. You're helping someone in a jam.

But let's say that the friend comes back the following month asking for more money without paying you back. And then again the next month. Your friend continually asks you for help paying their rent, but you notice that he's still going out to dinner all the time. Whenever you visit, you see Amazon boxes piled up in his front hall and he tells you about his newest hobby. He doesn't seem to be taking any steps to address his role in his financial issues. When you point this out, he becomes defensive and accuses you of being judgmental.

This is an obvious case of underfunctioning. The friend is not taking ownership of the responsibilities on his side of the boundary line—his debts, financial literacy, bank account. It can be very painful to see someone you love underfunction, especially in such serious areas of life.

When this friend asks again for money, how can you respond with boundaries? And more important, is there a way you can meet your responsibilities to help a friend without overfunctioning?

Assessing our own boundaries requires an honest look at our own internal motivations and responsibilities. With that in mind, here are some examples of how you might overfunction in this scenario:

Example 1:

You continue to give your friend money each month because you are afraid he will be upset with you if you say no. So, you decide to give it to him to prevent the pain and discomfort of telling him no. Resentment builds and the relationship is strained.

Example 2:

You fear that if you do not keep paying his rent, he might be evicted or even lose his home. So, you continue to give him money. You are preventing your friend from experiencing the consequences of their actions to avoid the pain of witnessing it. But in doing so, you also rob your friend of an opportunity to learn from his mistakes.

Example 3:

You continue to offer financial support because feeling liked and being seen as a generous person soothes your insecurities or sensitivities. But we already know that the hard work of developing a healthy self-concept falls on our side of the boundary line—and can't be fixed by controlling others, no matter how kind the deed.

Even if you genuinely wanted to help your friend, notice how in all these scenarios, your decisions center on your desire to avoid emotional discomfort, rather than what is best for your friend and yourself. That's not a boundaried way to make decisions and is unlikely to lead to helpful outcomes for your friend or a better relationship between the two of you.

What would happen if you stopped making decisions as though you were responsible *for* this friend, which leads to overfunctioning, and instead focused on making decisions that honored your responsibilities to this person?

If you were to take a moment to write down what are and are not your responsibilities to your friend in this situation, it might look like this:

Because this is a close friend with whom I have an interdependent relationship,

- I have a responsibility to listen and be supportive emotionally.

- I have a responsibility to offer practical help if I have the physical and mental bandwidth for it.

- I have a responsibility to be honest with my friend in a manner that takes his feelings into consideration.

- I have a responsibility to hold him accountable.

- Because this is not a minor or a co-parent, I do not have a responsibility to financially support him.

- It's not my responsibility to protect him from the consequences of his poor financial decisions.

- It's not my responsibility to guilt-trip him into changing his behavior, but neither is it my responsibility to protect him from feeling guilt about his decisions.

Taking that into consideration, here are some ways you could help your friend that are not overfunctioning but honor your responsibilities. Which one you ultimately choose will depend on your comfort level and your other responsibilities:

Example 1:

You can stop giving money and express your concerns to your friend about the way his financial decisions are impacting his life and your relationship. You carefully consider whether you have the bandwidth or ability to offer practical support. If you do, you can offer practical advice that isn't monetary like a lead on jobs in the area or an offer to help them write a résumé or build a budget.

Example 2:

You can give him money one more time (if it doesn't prevent you from meeting your own financial obligations) to give him time to get his affairs in order. Instead of giving the money to him directly, offer to send a check directly to the landlord so you are sure it gets used for rent. Use the opportunity to express your concerns.

Example 3:

You can also decide to just keep giving him money. If you've done these steps and still feel you have a valid reason for providing financial assistance, and that assistance does not compromise your other responsibilities, continue. I couldn't possibly cover every nuance that might apply to your relationships. Boundaries aren't about deciding who is deserving and who isn't. They aren't about rigidly refusing to do anything beyond the minimum responsibilities. Boundaries are about allowing us to give in ways that don't harm ourselves or others and allow us to show up for people authentically.

THEIR RENT PAYMENT

THEIR DECISION NOT
    TO PAY RENT

THE CONSEQUENCES
    OF THEIR DECISION

THEIR FEELINGS
ABOUT MY REFUSAL

THEIR BELIEFS
ABOUT MY INTENTIONS

BOUNDARIES ALLOW US TO SEE
WE ARE GIVING TOO MUCH OR
FOR ALL THE WRONG REASONS.
IT'S NOT ABOUT CONTROLLING
SOMEONE ELSE'S BEHAVIOR, BUT
ABOUT SETTING LIMITS ON OUR OWN.

the takeaway:

Overfunctioning isn't about other people but about a lack of internal boundaries. Overfunctioning can manifest in all kinds of behavior, including people-pleasing and enabling, which require a hard look at our own side of the responsibilities chart.

ultimatums and boundaries

Sometimes an ultimatum is an empty threat,
but sometimes it's an appropriate heads-up.

Perhaps the Decision Tree has helped you clarify that unless some things can change in your relationship, the right thing to do will be to disengage. Perhaps you are in the stage where you are disappointed by how the other person is responding to your boundaries and invitations to collaborate on solutions. Or perhaps they've committed to a course of action, but you are seeing signs that they're not really willing to follow through.

At this point, you may be tempted to make an ultimatum. An ultimatum can refer to a specific decision within a relationship, like "We won't be coming to Christmas if Dad keeps drinking," or it could mean a decision to end a relationship entirely. Ultimatums get a bad rap, but the truth is ultimatums aren't inherently bad or good. It all depends on how and why you use them.

In some cases, an ultimatum can be an expression of a boundary. In other cases, an ultimatum may be nothing more than a control tactic.

Boundaries are about controlling your own behavior. Control tactics are about trying to control someone else's. Control tactics aren't always used with malicious intent. We often try to control others out of genuinely good motives. (I once heard of a family that promised their adult son five thousand dollars if he would just complete rehab—that's about control.)

In the example that ended the Decision Tree section, Stephen, who discovered that his wife had another affair after nearly breaking up because of an earlier transgression, decided he had a responsibility to work things out with his wife. He chose to stay in the relationship but gave Lola an ultimatum: Cheat again and he would break off the marriage. So, is this ultimatum a boundary or a control tactic?

It depends.

Let's look at the difference between boundaries and control tactics.

Boundaries	Control Tactics
When your actions are designed to protect your health and sanity.	When your actions are designed to get someone to change their behavior.
When you communicate what you are or aren't going to do.	When you use threats and orders that are designed to instill fear of repercussion.
When you follow through on ultimatums regardless of what the other person does.	When you use empty threats and don't follow through when the other person continues their behavior.

Boundaries	Control Tactics
When you refuse to participate in someone else's self-destructive behavior.	When you justify participating in someone else's self-destructive behaviors.
When you admit that you are powerless to control someone else's behavior and that you can only control your own.	When you believe that you can influence the ultimate outcome if you try hard enough.
When you act out of love, even if it appears to the other person to be a betrayal.	When you appear to act out of love but are really causing harm.

Now, an ultimatum certainly *can* be a control tactic. Many times, we give ultimatums because we are desperate to make someone change. If Stephen is threatening to leave because he thinks that an ultimatum will be the thing that "finally gets through" to Lola and will force her to stop cheating and save their marriage, then it is not a boundary, it's a control tactic. If he isn't truly ready or willing to end the relationship if she cheats again, then it's a control tactic. Ultimatums born out of an effort to change others don't work in the long run. In my experience, people who make ultimatums before doing the important work around understanding their responsibilities with boundaries typically do not follow through with the threat.

That doesn't mean that ultimatums *can't* be boundaries. If Stephen were to give this ultimatum as a true boundary it would look like this: He would recognize that he has no control over Lola's behavior, and he cannot make her heal and change regardless of how much he loves her. The pain Stephen experiences because of Lola's behavior is overwhelming—not just the betrayal but also having to watch her self-destruct. He knows he cannot go on like this, that he must separate himself from the betrayal—and he hopes Lola will, too, so they can be together. But if she can't or won't, he will have to do it without her. This is having boundaries.

What would it look like for Lola to have boundaries? One of the hardest boundary lessons is that a great many things that are not your fault are now your responsibility. Mental health disorders, addiction, ADHD—none of those things are anyone's fault—but their impact on your life and your behavior is your responsibility to manage. Your sensitivities may result from childhood trauma or abuse, but the present-day effect is something you have to actively address. Lola becoming boundaried will mean recognizing her own responsibilities to address her trauma without making it an excuse to continue harmful behavior.

the takeaway:

Not all ultimatums are the same: Some come from a boundaried place and can be an effective tool to use in relationships. Others, when used to coerce, are control tactics and will not be helpful or effective in the long run.

using boundaries to stay or disengage

*You are not required
to set yourself on fire
to keep someone else warm.*

Now that you have a good concept of boundaries, let's see what it looks like to carry out the decision to stay or disengage from a relationship using boundaries.

First, I will take you through a series of questions with specific examples to follow to help clarify the concepts. Write your answers down on a piece of paper or use the template on page 207.

Answer each question the best you can.

1. What feelings are you having about this relationship?

2. What are your fears about this relationship?

3. Write down one hard truth about the situation and one comforting truth.

4.   In the middle of the page, draw a boundary line down the middle. On the left side, write out the feelings, fears, decisions, and obligations you are responsible for. On the right side, write down the feelings, fears, decisions, and obligations the other person is responsible for.

5.   Write down your responsibilities to this person and any other people affected. Include both the standard lists from pages 182–183 and any additional ones that are unique to your situation.

6.   Think of options that allow you to act from your position in the boundary line while still communicating wants and needs in the manner that you feel is safe and warranted. Brainstorm changes you can make that honor your boundaries, your safety, and your well-being while allowing you to act with integrity according to what you feel is your responsibility to this person or others that might be affected.

Be sure to get feedback from your Advisory Team!
Let's apply this list to a few examples.

1. I FEEL ...

2. I AM AFRAID THAT ...

3. ONE HARD (TRUTH ↓)   **& ONE COMFORTING (TRUTH ↓)**

4. THE BOUNDARY ...

THINGS IN THIS RELATIONSHIP I AM RESPONSIBLE FOR MANAGING:

THINGS IN THIS RELATIONSHIP THEY ARE RESPONSIBLE FOR MANAGING:

5. MY RESPONSIBILITIES TO THIS PERSON (AND ANY OTHERS AFFECTED):

☐ _____   ☐ _____
☐ _____   ☐ _____

6. BRAINSTORMING BOUNDARIED DECISIONS:

a daughter's addiction

background

For years, Amiah's adult daughter Kylie has been struggling with addiction. Kylie's actions have had a destructive impact on Amiah's mental health, their relationship, and the stability of their home, where they live with Amiah's two younger children. Most recently, Kylie pawned Amiah's wedding ring to buy cocaine. Kylie is unwilling to get help for her addiction, so Amiah has decided she needs to put some distance between them to protect herself and her other children. Here is a look at how Amiah decides how to disengage with boundaries.

1. **What feelings are you having about this relationship?**

    I feel angry at my daughter and myself for letting it get this bad. I feel sad she is killing herself. I can't stand to watch it. I would do anything to help her. But I feel afraid in my house when she is here. I'm so sad and angry when I see how scared and sad my other children are because of Kylie's addiction.

2. **What are your fears about this relationship?**

    I'm afraid if I tell her she can't come here she will feel abandoned and will turn even more to drugs. But maybe if I told her she couldn't visit it would make her get sober. I'm so afraid of making the wrong choice and just so afraid she will die.

3. **Write down one hard truth and one comforting truth.**

    I cannot control my daughter's addiction. I am here in this pain, and I will survive it.

4.   The boundary

1. Things I am responsible for managing:

My safety, the safety of my other kids, my anger, my fears, who I allow to live in my house, my mental health, my reactions to Kylie.

2. Things Kylie is responsible for managing:

Her addiction, her decisions to break the law, the consequences of her theft, her behavior, her recovery, the feelings she has about my boundaries, her relationships with her sisters, her finances, her mental health.

5.   What are my responsibilities to this relationship?

To be honest, to be kind, to confront, to always love her, to never give up on her, to be there for her, to support her, to let her know she is loved, to show empathy to her.

6.   Brainstorm changes you can make that honor your boundaries, your safety, and your well-being.

Kylie is not a minor anymore, and I don't have a responsibility to give her a place to live, especially when she is in active addiction. My responsibility for my safety and the safety and well-being of my other kids means I can't have someone stealing or using in the house. My fear of how Kylie will react to this is something I have to deal with. How Kylie feels and thinks about this decision is not mine to control or fix.

I do have a responsibility to love Kylie and do what I can to communicate that love. Here are some ways I can do that that do not compromise my safety, well-being, or other responsibilities, and are not overfunctioning on her behalf:

1.   *On months when I can afford it, I can take her to the grocery store and buy her some food. It's not my responsibility to feed her, and it won't get her sober, but it's something kind I can do to show her I'm always going to be here for her. It's also better than giving her money because if I give her money, I know she will spend it on drugs.*

2.   *I can give her a list of phone numbers to call when she decides to get clean and let her know I will come to any family visitation or therapy.*

3.   *I have to be honest with Kylie and tell her how hurt I am that she stole my ring. I know it won't make her stop using, but it's important to be honest with her about the impact of her actions.*

a friend who can't reciprocate

background

Laura and her best friend, Chanel, have been inseparable since childhood. However, in the past few years, Chanel has struggled with her mental health. She goes through periods of depression where she isolates and doesn't reach out or answer Laura's calls for months. Laura knows her friend isn't intending to be hurtful, but it's very painful to have a best friend who often disappears and can't be there for her when she needs her. After going through the Decision Tree, Laura has decided that she will stay in a friendship with Chanel, but she needs to enact some boundaries to protect her well-being.

1. **What feelings are you having about this relationship?**

   I feel angry and sad that my best friend can't support me. I've done everything to show her she is loved and to cheer her up, but I can't get through to her. How do I make her see? I feel so alone when she goes radio silent. I'm struggling, too.

2. **What are your fears about this relationship?**

   I'm scared Chanel will never get better and we will never be the friends we used to be who could support each other. I'm scared if I make new friendships, Chanel will feel left behind and it will make her depression worse.

3. **Write down one hard truth and one comforting truth.**

   Chanel may never be the kind of friend I need her to be again. It's okay to grieve the relationship I wish we had, it doesn't make me a bad person.

4.   The boundary

1.   Things I am responsible for managing:

My anger, my sadness, my fears, my need for support, my need for connection.

2.   Things Chanel is responsible for managing:

Her mental health, her coping skills, her communication skills, her willingness to reach out for help.

5.   What are your responsibilities to this relationship?

To be honest, to show empathy, to confront when necessary, to be authentic and vulnerable.

6.   Brainstorm changes you can make that honor your boundaries, your safety, and your well-being.

My responsibility to show empathy means I don't want to shame her for something I know comes from her depression. She is a great friend when she is well, but it's really hard for me to suddenly have no friend support. I want to support and help my friend, but I also need support—so I don't think right now she is a friend I can go to for the support I need. I can keep in touch with her and reach out to support her any way I can, but I need to find other friends that are in a more stable place to get the support I need. It makes me sad to know we may not be as close, and I can't control whether she feels upset that I've made new friends, but this is the only way I can think of to take care of myself and be a good friend to her.

a hobby that becomes a headache

background

Lilly's partner, Gill, has always been an avid cyclist. His six-hour Saturday hobby wasn't an issue until they had children. Now, Lilly has given up many of her hobbies to care for their new baby, but Gill has continued his Saturday cycling, leaving Lilly to care for the baby on her own. Lilly has tried to talk to Gill about what she views is inequity in their relationship and invite him to collaborate on ways to make things feel more equal, like taking shorter rides or making time for Lilly to have comparable time away for self-care, but Gill continues his rides. Unfortunately, it appears Gill isn't really willing to change anything. When Lilly used the Decision Tree, it led her to the answer that she ought to give herself permission to leave this relationship. Despite knowing she could leave, she just isn't ready to make such a huge change. So, she is exploring ways to protect her well-being with boundaries.

1.   What feelings are you having about this relationship?

I feel overwhelmed and angry that Gill does not see how selfish he is being. I want him to stay home and stop cycling so he can help me. I need a break, too! He gets to leave every Saturday, but whenever I ask for one he makes me feel like I'm putting him out. I've talked to him about this a thousand times, and he doesn't get it. It's really painful when Gill acts like I'm unreasonable.

2.   What are your fears about this relationship?

I'm afraid that if I leave this relationship I'll never survive as a single mom. I'm scared that if I push for more time to care for myself, Gill will judge me and think I'm being dramatic and unreasonable.

3.   **Write down one hard truth about the situation and one comforting truth.**

There is nothing I can do to make Gill willing to see the inequity in our relationship. But it's not my job to manage Gill's perception of my needs. It's my job to take care of me.

4.   **The boundary**

   1.   **Things I am responsible for managing:**
        My mental health, being whole for my daughter, speaking up for what I need, my decisions, my feelings.

   2.   **Things Gill is responsible for managing:**
        His decision to cycle, his understanding of my needs, his perception of our relationship, his willingness to change, his commitment to being an equal parent, his insight into his behavior.

5.   **What are your responsibilities to this relationship?**

I'm responsible for being respectful when I communicate with Gill and at this point that's about it.

6.   **Brainstorm changes you can make that honor your boundaries, your safety, and your well-being.**

If I don't get a break I am going to lose my mind. I can't control what Gill does. But I can control what I do. I can be honest about the impact his behavior has on me and tell him I think it's going to jeopardize our relationship if we don't find a way for me to also get breaks.

I'm going to tell Gill that from now on, I will be going to a book club on Thursday nights. He won't like it, but he cares for our daughter and won't put her in danger if he must watch her. I am also going to hire a mother's helper to come Saturday mornings to help me when Gill is cycling.

If he isn't going to stop cycling on Saturdays and he isn't going to suddenly offer to give me a break, I can tell him that from now on if he cycles every Saturday then I will go out every Sunday. He will sulk about it. That makes me feel anxious and guilty but I know I am not doing anything wrong and it's not my job to manage his feelings about it. It is my responsibility to be healthy and whole for my child.

I can put forth the effort to work on this issue with Gill, and if the dynamic doesn't change, I can come up with new boundaries or revisit my Decision Tree.

the takeaway:

Working with a definition of boundaries that are internally motivated by your responsibilities to yourself and to others, you can begin using this framework to help clarify and strengthen the outcome of your Decision Tree.

boundaries and abuse

Oh, dear heart, it wasn't your fault.

Can having strong boundaries help you navigate a situation where abuse is present? Absolutely.

It's important to remember there is no boundary that can control someone who is dead set on violating you. You cannot become so boundaried that you can prevent someone from doing you intentional harm.

When you are dealing with abuse dynamics, having boundaries does not involve acting authentically or vulnerably or even honestly if it means your physical or psychological safety is compromised.

In situations where you are victimized, having boundaries means that you assign blame to the person to whom it belongs—the one doing the harmful behavior. You could not have controlled their behavior and so you will not wear the shame.

The shame of rape belongs to a rapist.
The guilt of abuse belongs to the abuser.

An abuser can violate your body, your trust, your autonomy, even your dignity. These are deep wounds. They can create deep wells of grief that require substantial support. But the one thing an abuser cannot do is assign their guilt to *you*. They cannot force you to wear their shame. They cannot transfer the responsibility of their violation to you. It remains with them until they settle up with their maker. Knowing this fact, you have two choices: You can whisper under your breath, "May God have mercy on their soul," or you can scream from the mountains, "Fuck their soul, I hope if there is a god, he bathes in your blood."

Either response is permissible. You are not responsible for giving your abuser forgiveness. Your only responsibility is to yourself—to find safety, to rebuild, to heal. To find peace. Sometimes forgiveness brings that. But only when it's chosen. Never when it's obligated.

Plenty of people find peace without forgiveness. Sometimes the path forward is "I deserve to be free of you completely—even from the intimacy of hating you."

the takeaway:

Boundaries are necessary in healthy and functioning relationships—and they are also essential to navigating abusive ones.

the great relay

Some parents who hurt their children
are malicious sociopaths.
Some are not.
This chapter is about the latter.

In the mind of a young child, there are no boundaries between them and their parents. Mother and child are quite literally one entity for the first nine months of cellular existence. Children don't even register that their caregivers are separate beings from them until they are several months old. For years into childhood, they live in a state of "prolonged helplessness" where their nervous system regulation is dependent upon their caregiver's. A caregiver's stress stresses the child and a caregiver's calm calms them.

Young children cannot conceptualize their parents as having a life outside themselves. When parents hurt their kids, intentionally or not, children don't have the boundaries to say, "Oh my parent must have had a stressful day at work." Instead, they think, "I've done something to displease my parent." In otherwise healthy parent-child relationships, where there is enough unconditional love and ruptures are repaired, these moments become opportunities to strengthen trust and learn boundaries. But when a child is repeatedly mistreated, they will fold into shame, internalizing unlovability.

As children grow, they fully differentiate from their parents. They realize that no, the mistreatment was not their fault. In fact, it was unfair. They didn't deserve that. And many times, they feel angry at their parents for how much harm they caused.

Then a child becomes an adult and they are forced to look at their own relationships and identify the wounds their parents gave them and the sensitivities that drive defense mechanisms that create cycles that hurt loved ones.

Until one day it hits them: Parents have wounds, too. Wounds that they may have incurred when the world harmed them. They were just children—it wasn't their fault. In fact, it was unfair. They didn't deserve that, either.

They didn't deserve that.
And that makes us sad.
But neither did we.
And that still makes us angry.

Both truths can exist together.

My relationship with my father in my childhood left me deeply wounded because he was wounded. He has acknowledged the pain he caused me and has asked for forgiveness, despite never receiving any apology from the ones who hurt him.

And, reader, I have decided to end this cycle. I've given him my forgiveness.

Just because our parents didn't break *all* the generational curses, doesn't mean they didn't break some of them. And maybe I won't break them all, either—but I'll work to break more of them than my father did with the hope that my children will continue this work.

Ultimately, maybe that's what we are all here for—to take turns each kicking the can down the road, a little farther each time.

citations and further resources

introduction

emotional abuse of children

For more information on emotional abuse of children, visit:

https://www.nspcc.org.uk/what-is-child-abuse/types-of-abuse
/emotional-abuse/

https://childsafety.losangelescriminallawyer.pro/kids-and
-emotional-psychological-abuse.html

https://www.parentingforbrain.com/emotionally-abusive-parents/

getting help with abusive relationships

For a list of warning signes of abuse, visit https://www.thehotline.org
/identify-abuse/domestic-abuse-warning-signs

To speak privately with an advocate and get help, visit thehotline.org,
call 1-800-799-7233, or text START to 88788.

Visit the National Domestic Violence Hotline website at www.thehotline
.org for more signs and symptoms of relationship abuse, including

physical abuse, emotional abuse, sexual abuse, sexual coercion, financial abuse, reproductive coercion, and digital abuse.

To create a personalized safety plan and find a list of resources in your area, visit www.thehotline.org/plan-for-safety/create-your-personal-safety-plan/.

chapter 2: building your advisory team

books on how to build friendships and community

Platonic: How the Science of Attachment Can Help You Make—and Keep—Friends by Marisa G. Franco, PhD

Find Your People: Building Deep Community in a Lonely World by Jennie Allen

Loneliness: Human Nature and the Need for Social Connection by John T. Cacioppo and William Patrick

chapter 3: the vulnerability cycle

the vulnerability cycle

The Vulnerability Cycle is a concept created by Michele Scheinkman, CSW, and Mona DeKoven Fishbane, PhD.

Scheinkman, Michele, and Mona DeKoven Fishbane. "The Vulnerability Cycle: Working with Impasses in Couple Therapy."

Family Process 43, no. 3 (2004): 279–99. https://doi.org/10.1111 /j.1545-5300.2004.00023.x.

chapter 4: how to slow down the vulnerability cycle

communication during conflict

For a short but excellent guide on how to better communicate during conflict, check out:

How to Have the Best Fight of Your Life: A Therapist's Blueprint for Resolving Conflict and Finding Your Way Back to the One You Love by Lindley Gentile, LMFT, and Jess Worthington, LMFT

chapter 5: how emotional dysregulation fuels the vulnerability cycle

window of tolerance

Dr. Daniel J. Siegel, a clinical professor of psychiatry at UCLA, developed the concept of the window of tolerance and the "hand model" of the brain, which discusses the interplay between the survival brain and the thinking brain. You can see his work at drdansiegel.com.

Dr. Dan Siegel's Hand Model of the Brain, https://drdansiegel.com /hand-model-of-the-brain/

chapter 6: how to emotionally regulate

nervous system interventions

Research for interventions in this chapter can be found at:

Breathing exercises: Balban, Melis Yilmaz, Eric Neri, Manuela M. Kogon, et al. "Brief Structured Respiration Practices Enhance Mood and Reduce Physiological Arousal." *Cell Reports Medicine* 4, no. 1 (2023): 100895. https://www.cell.com/cell-reports -medicine/fulltext/S2666-3791(22)00474-8.

Icing the vagus nerve: Mäkinen, Tiina M., Matti Mäntysaari, Tiina Pääkkönen, et al. "Autonomic Nervous Function During Whole-Body Cold Exposure Before and After Cold Acclimation." *Aviation, Space, and Environmental Medicine* 79, no. 9 (2008): 875–82. https://doi.org/10.3357/asem.2235.2008.

Humming for emotional regulation: Vickhoff, Björn, Helge Malmgren, Rickard Åström, et al. "Music Structure Determines Heart Rate Variability of Singers." *Frontiers in Psychology* 4 (2013). https://doi .org/10.3389/fpsyg.2013.00334.

additional resources:

For more exercises to reduce physiological arousal, check out *The Anxiety Healer's Guide* by Alison Seponara, MS, LPC.

More self-compassion exercises by Dr. Kristen Neff can be found at https://self-compassion.org/.

For deeper exercises on learning the skills of emotional regulation and distress tolerance, check out *The Dialectical Behavior Therapy Skills Workbook: Practical DBT Exercises for Learning Mindfulness, Interpersonal Effectiveness, Emotion Regulation, and Distress Tolerance* by Matthew McKay, PhD, Jeffrey C. Wood, PsyD, and Jeffrey Brantley, MD.

chapter 8: the relationship decision tree

how divorce affects children

Government of Canada, Department of Justice, Electronic Communications. Studies of High Conflict and Its Effect on Children - "High-Conflict Separation and Divorce: Options for Consideration" (2004-FCY-1E) (2015). https://www.justice.gc.ca /eng/rp-pr/fl-lf/divorce/2004_1/p3.html.

Cao, Hongjian, Mark A. Fine, and Nan Zhou. "The Divorce Process and Child Adaptation Trajectory Typology (DPCATT) Model: The Shaping Role of Predivorce and Postdivorce Interparental Conflict." *Clinical Child and Family Psychology Review* 25, no. 3 (2022): 500–28. https://doi.org/10.1007/s10567-022-00379-3.

chapter 10: why the small moments matter

the gottman institute

For more information on John and Julie Gottman's research on bids and other marriage topics, visit https://www.gottman.com/.

additional resources

sexual dynamics in relationships

Mating in Captivity: Reconciling the Erotic and the Domestic by Esther Perel

division of labor

Fair Play: A Game-Changing Solution for When You Have Too Much to Do (and More Life to Live) by Eve Rodsky

acknowledgments

I would like to acknowledge all the brilliant minds who helped me make this book possible.

To all my colleagues, I am humbled and thankful for the official and unofficial consultations—the phone calls, the Zooms, the late-night texting, the brainstorming, and the sharing of your time, your talent, and your insight: I am specially thankful to Lindley Gentile, LMFT, for her incredible insight into the Vulnerability Cycle; Lesley Cook, PsyD, for her expertise on emotional regulation; Derrick Hoard, LMFT, for his knowledge on relational dynamics; Soo Jin Lee, LMFT, and Linda Yoon, LCSW, for helping me craft thoughtful examples that honor their heritage; Heidi Smith, LPC-S, for teaching me everything she knows about boundaries.

A huge thank-you to my friends and family who let me bounce ideas off them and who told me whether I was making a lick of sense, especially Ollie Rose, Katie Walton, and my dear sister Kelly Allen. Thank you to my agents Kim Witherspoon and Jessica Mileo for always believing in me, and to Doris Cooper, Richard Rhorer, Jessica Preeg, Elizabeth Breeden, Maria Espinosa, and everyone at Simon Element for being such a supportive and amazing team. And to Susannah Cahalan for helping me bring this book across the finish line.

Lastly, I would like to thank my mom, whose love has kept me even in my darkest days; my precious daughters, who are the light of my life; and Michael, who remains the greatest love of my life.

about the author

KC Davis is the bestselling author of *How to Keep House While Drowning*. A licensed therapist, she is the creator of the popular Struggle Care website and Instagram page, and the Domestic Blisters TikTok, where she shares her revolutionary approach to self- and home care for those dealing with mental health issues, physical illness, and hard seasons of life. Across platforms, KC has more than 1.6 million followers. KC has been featured in *The Washington Post*, *Oprah Daily*, *Slate*, *Well+Good*, *Good Inside with Dr. Becky*, and *Ten Percent Happier with Dan Harris*, among dozens of other media. She recently launched the podcast *Struggle Care*, which is available on every podcast platform. She lives in Houston with her husband and two daughters.